THE ULTIMATE
HUMAN BODY
ENCYCLOPEDIA

Published in 2022 by Welbeck Children's
An Imprint of Welbeck Children's Limited,
part of the Welbeck Publishing Group
Offices in: London - 20 Mortimer Street, London W1T 3JW
& Sydney - 205 Commonwealth Street, Surry Hills 2010
www.welbeckpublishing.com

A CIP catalogue record for this book is available from the British Library.

Author: Jon Richards
Consultant: Penny Johnson
Layout and design: Tall Tree Ltd
Editorial Director: Joff Brown
Design Manager: Matt Drew
Production: Melanie Robertson

ISBN 978 1 78312 990 4

Printed in Heshan, China

10 9 8 7 6 5 4 3 2 1

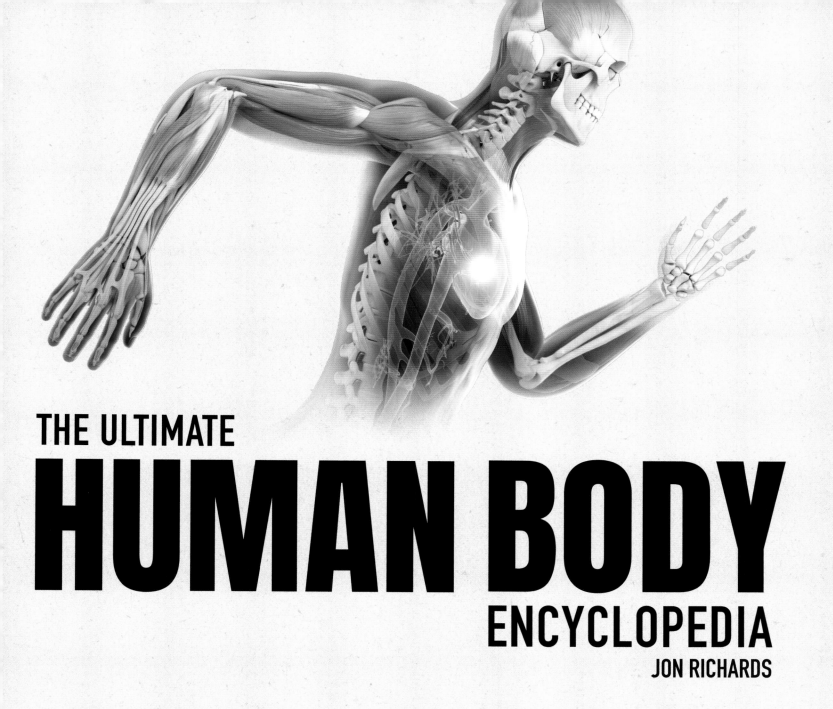

THE ULTIMATE
HUMAN BODY
ENCYCLOPEDIA
JON RICHARDS

The complete visual guide to how your body works

WELBECK

CONTENTS

INTRODUCTION
ORGANISING THE BODY

The human body is an amazing structure that allows you to move about, sense the world, communicate with other people and grow from a small baby into a full-size adult. Beneath the surface is a very complicated array of tiny cells, tissues, organs and systems that work together to make all of this possible.

CELLS
Cells are tiny living building blocks and they come in lots of different shapes and sizes depending on the job they have to do.

NERVE CELLS
These have long, thin strands that carry nerve signals around your body.

RED BLOOD CELLS
These are shaped like discs and they carry oxygen to your body's cells and help to carry waste carbon dioxide away.

MUSCLE CELLS
These have special fibres that contract (get shorter) to pull on different body parts.

TISSUES
Similar cells join together to form tissues to carry out a particular function. For example, nerve cells join together to form nervous tissue, while muscle cells join together to form muscle tissue.

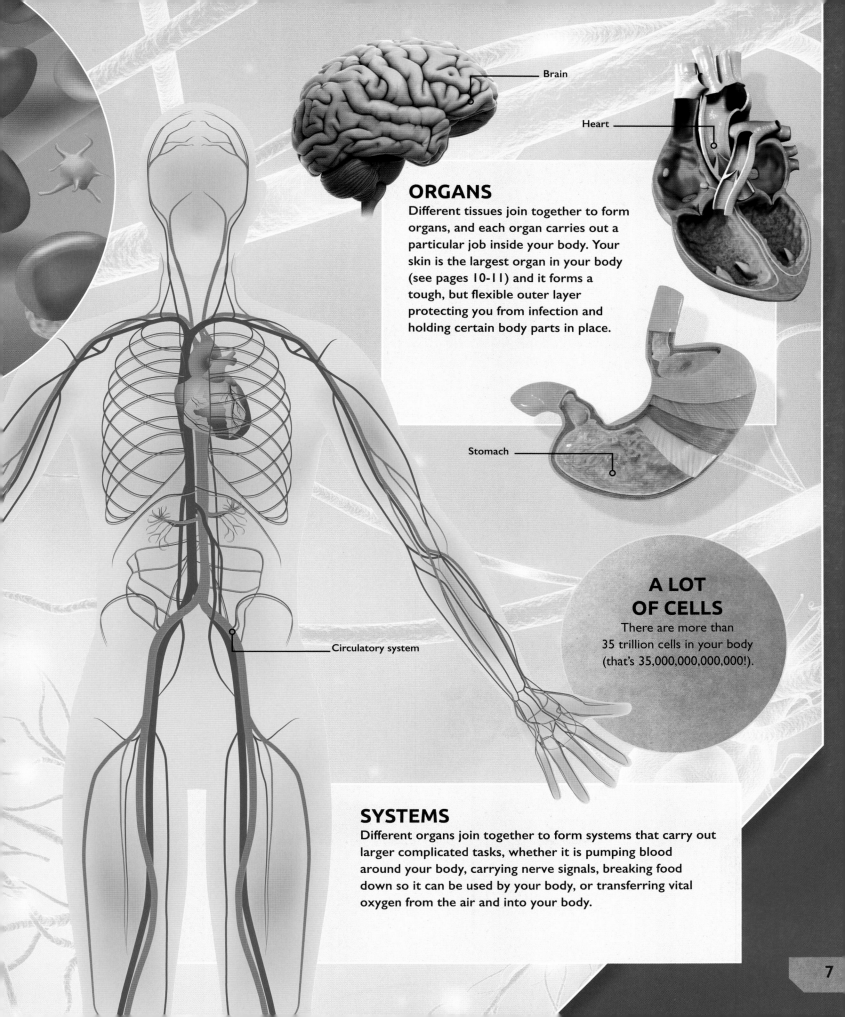

Brain

Heart

ORGANS

Different tissues join together to form organs, and each organ carries out a particular job inside your body. Your skin is the largest organ in your body (see pages 10-11) and it forms a tough, but flexible outer layer protecting you from infection and holding certain body parts in place.

Stomach

Circulatory system

A LOT OF CELLS

There are more than 35 trillion cells in your body (that's 35,000,000,000,000!).

SYSTEMS

Different organs join together to form systems that carry out larger complicated tasks, whether it is pumping blood around your body, carrying nerve signals, breaking food down so it can be used by your body, or transferring vital oxygen from the air and into your body.

BODY STRUCTURE
SKIN, SKELETON AND MUSCLES

The outer layer of the human body is formed of the skin, hair and nails, which together are known as the integumentary system. Almost every part of the human body that you can see on the outside is formed from dead cells. These are filled with a hard material called keratin, which creates a tough layer that protects the body from damage and infection.

Under the skin are hundreds of hard bones and softer cartilage that make up the skeletal system. These vary in shape and size, from the tiny ossicles found inside the ears to the long bones that make up the legs and arms, and from the tough shell of the skull to the small rods that are found in the fingers and toes. Together, the bones and cartilage act as levers for the muscles to pull on, protect certain body parts and support the entire body.

The skeletal muscles are made from a special tissue that can contract, pulling on body parts to move arms and legs, turn the head from side to side, and make a whole range of other movements.

Without muscles, you wouldn't be able to move your limbs, and without bones to pull on, the muscles would be floppy bits of tissue. Together, they allow the human body to perform a wide range of actions, including gymnastic vaults and tumbles.

SKIN AND NAILS

The skin is the largest organ in the human body. It wraps the body in a protective barrier that replaces itself regularly, helps to control temperature, helps to prevent infection and stops harmful substances getting inside.

UNDER THE SURFACE

The skin has two layers. The epidermis is at the top with the dermis beneath. At the bottom of the epidermis, skin cells divide and the new cells are pushed to the surface. As they rise, the cells become flatter and fill with a protein called keratin, making them tough and waterproof. When they reach the surface, they are rubbed off and worn away before being replaced by newer cells.

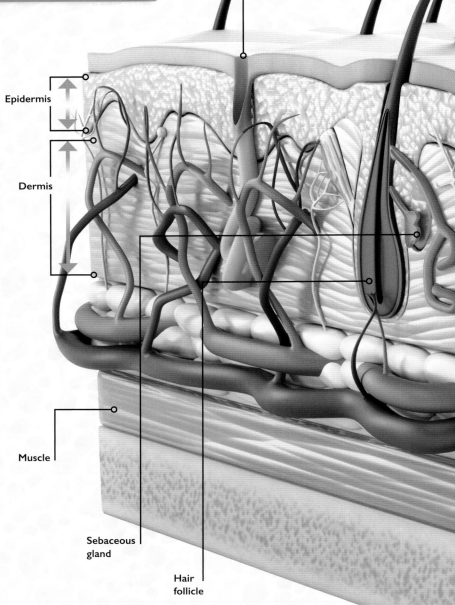

Hair

Sweat pore

Epidermis

Dermis

Muscle

Sebaceous gland

Hair follicle

KEEPING SKIN HEALTHY

The Sun's rays contain harmful forms of energy, such as ultraviolet rays, that can damage skin cells and cause cancers. The skin produces a pigment called melanin that can protect the skin from some damage. However, in very strong sunlight it's best to use a suitable sunscreen and wear hats and clothes that can block out these harmful forms of radiation.

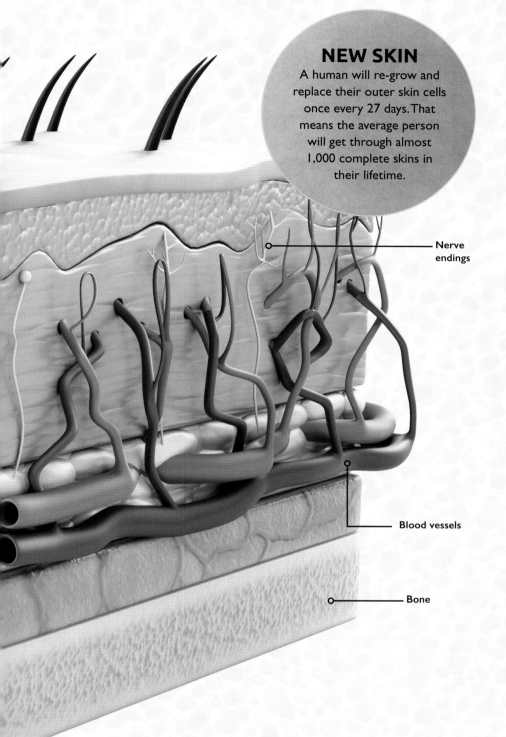

NEW SKIN

A human will re-grow and replace their outer skin cells once every 27 days. That means the average person will get through almost 1,000 complete skins in their lifetime.

Nerve endings

Blood vessels

Bone

TEMPERATURE CONTROL

When you get hot, blood vessels near the skin's surface enlarge (called vasodilation), so more blood moves to the surface of the skin to lose heat. At the same time, sweat glands produce more sweat, which evaporates from the body, taking heat with it.

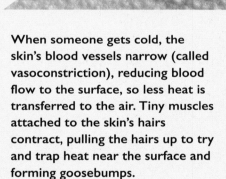

When someone gets cold, the skin's blood vessels narrow (called vasoconstriction), reducing blood flow to the surface, so less heat is transferred to the air. Tiny muscles attached to the skin's hairs contract, pulling the hairs up to try and trap heat near the surface and forming goosebumps.

NAILS

Nail cells divide from the matrix at the very bottom of the nail. As the cells are pushed forwards at about 3 mm every month, they fill with keratin, making them very hard. Nails help to support and protect the tips of the fingers and toes.

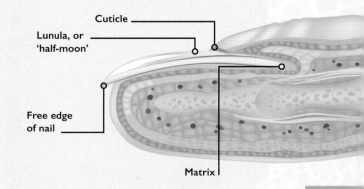

Cuticle

Lunula, or 'half-moon'

Free edge of nail

Matrix

HAIR

Human beings are mammals and have bodies covered in hair. This varies from the thick hair that may grow on the top of your head to the fine hairs that cover most of your body.

HEAD HAIR

The colour of the hair on your head depends on the amount and type of a pigment called melanin (the same pigment that colours the skin). Black hair has a lot of a type of melanin called eumelanin, while brown contains less of this pigment and blonde hair has very little. Red hair contains a different type of melanin called pheomelanin.

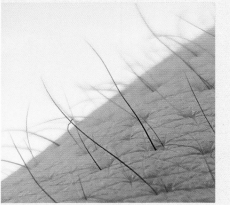

BODY HAIR

Most of your body is covered in a fine type of hair called vellus hairs. The only parts that do not have hairs on them are the palms of your hands, the soles of your feet, your lips and your nipples.

PUBIC HAIR

When a person reaches puberty, they will start to grow pubic hair around the genitals, and in their armpits. These hairs can trap dirt and bacteria, protecting these sensitive parts of the body, while the sebum produced by the sebaceous glands at the base of the hairs stops bacteria from reproducing.

FIGHTING INFECTION

Pus is a thick fluid that the body produces when fighting an infection. It contains dead cells and bacteria.

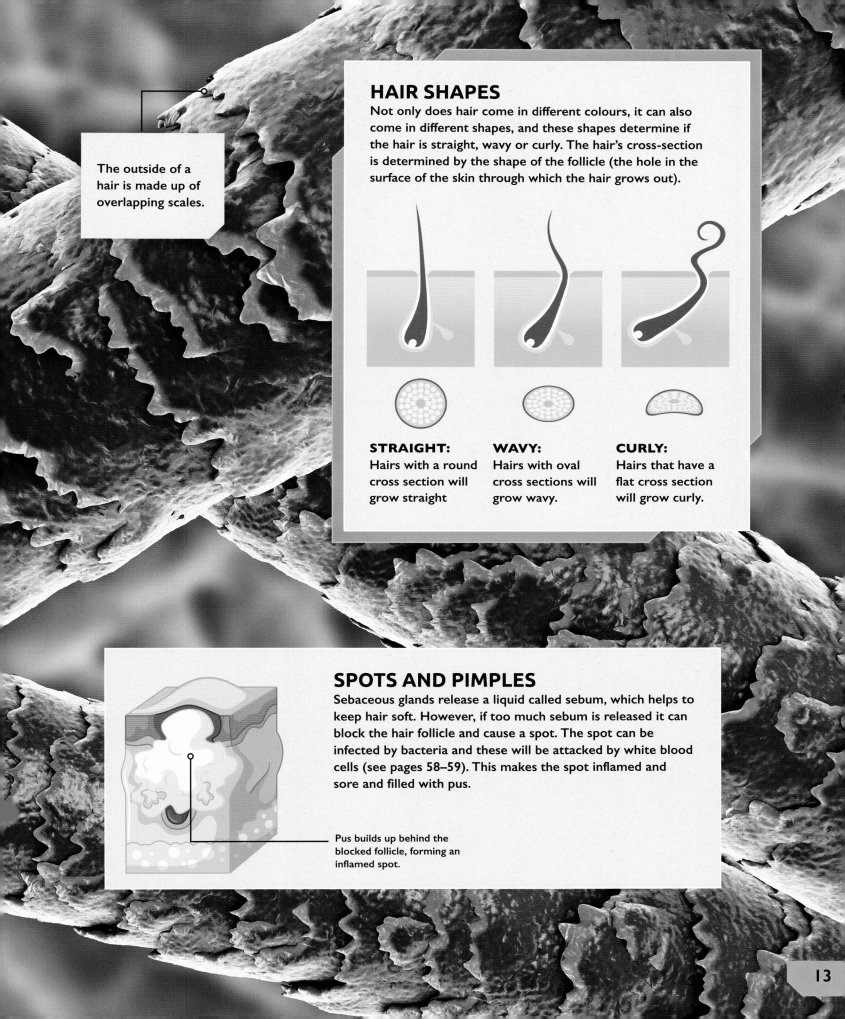

The outside of a hair is made up of overlapping scales.

HAIR SHAPES

Not only does hair come in different colours, it can also come in different shapes, and these shapes determine if the hair is straight, wavy or curly. The hair's cross-section is determined by the shape of the follicle (the hole in the surface of the skin through which the hair grows out).

STRAIGHT:
Hairs with a round cross section will grow straight

WAVY:
Hairs with oval cross sections will grow wavy.

CURLY:
Hairs that have a flat cross section will grow curly.

SPOTS AND PIMPLES

Sebaceous glands release a liquid called sebum, which helps to keep hair soft. However, if too much sebum is released it can block the hair follicle and cause a spot. The spot can be infected by bacteria and these will be attacked by white blood cells (see pages 58–59). This makes the spot inflamed and sore and filled with pus.

Pus builds up behind the blocked follicle, forming an inflamed spot.

THE SKELETON

Under the surface of your skin is a system of bones, which helps you to move about, holds you up and protect fragile parts of the body. This incredible framework is called the skeleton and, as well as keeping you upright, it gets bigger as you grow and can even heal itself if a bone breaks.

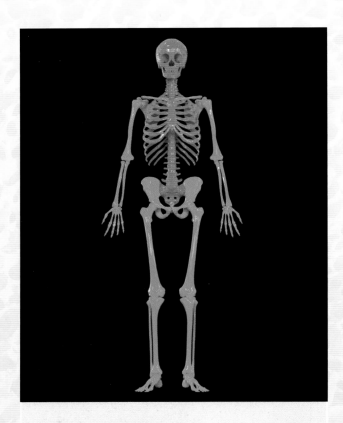

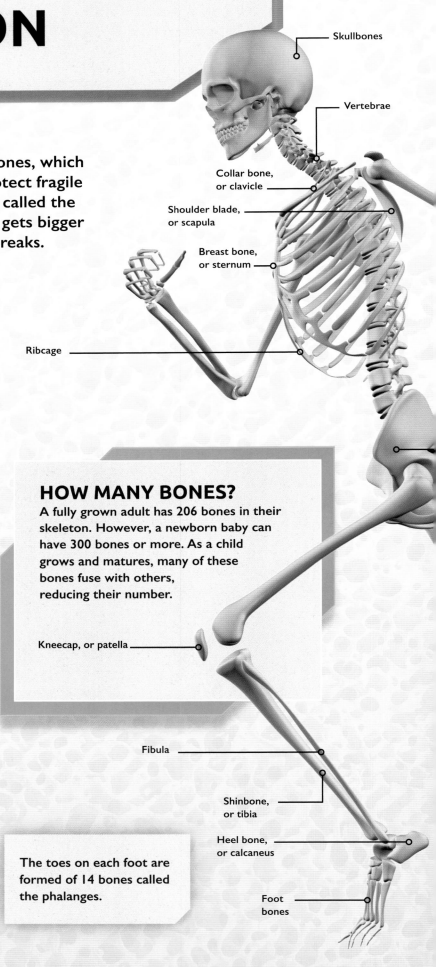

Skullbones

Vertebrae

Collar bone, or clavicle

Shoulder blade, or scapula

Breast bone, or sternum

Ribcage

HOW MANY BONES?

A fully grown adult has 206 bones in their skeleton. However, a newborn baby can have 300 bones or more. As a child grows and matures, many of these bones fuse with others, reducing their number.

Kneecap, or patella

TWO PARTS

Scientists divide the human skeleton into two parts. The central part is called the axial skeleton (shown red, above) and it is made up of the skull, the backbone, the ribs and the sternum (chest bone). Hanging off this is the appendicular skeleton (shown blue, above), which is made up of the pelvis, shoulder bones, arms, hands, legs and feet.

Fibula

Shinbone, or tibia

Heel bone, or calcaneus

The toes on each foot are formed of 14 bones called the phalanges.

Foot bones

SMALL BONES

The smallest bones in the skeleton are found inside the ears. Each ear has three tiny bones; the malleus, stapes and incus (together known as the ossicles).

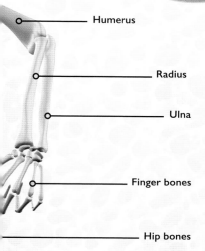

Humerus

Radius

Ulna

Finger bones

Hip bones

Thigh bone, or femur

SEEING THE SKELETON

Even though bones are inside the body, doctors can study them without having to cut someone open. X-rays, a high-energy form of radiation, can pass through soft tissues in the body, such as skin and muscle, but they are absorbed and blocked by bones. An image made using X-rays can reveal if a bone is broken (see pages 24–25) or not growing as it should.

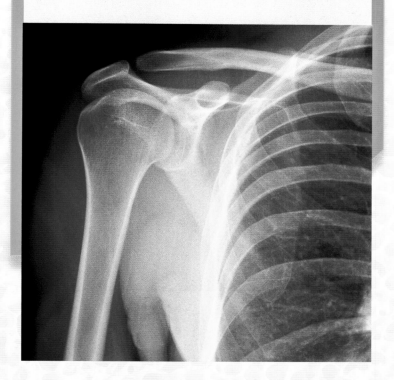

KEEPING BONES HEALTHY

During your lifetime your skeleton will undergo a lot of stress, so it's important to keep it healthy. Regular exercise will help to keep bone tissue dense and strong, while a diet that is high in both calcium and vitamin D will help to keep bones healthy. Calcium is a major component of bone tissue, while vitamin D helps the body absorb calcium from the food you eat.

BONE SHAPES

The 206 bones that make up the skeleton come in a range of shapes and sizes depending on the jobs they have to do. These include acting as levers to move limbs about, providing a wide, flat surface for muscles to attach to, protecting delicate organs or connecting other bones together.

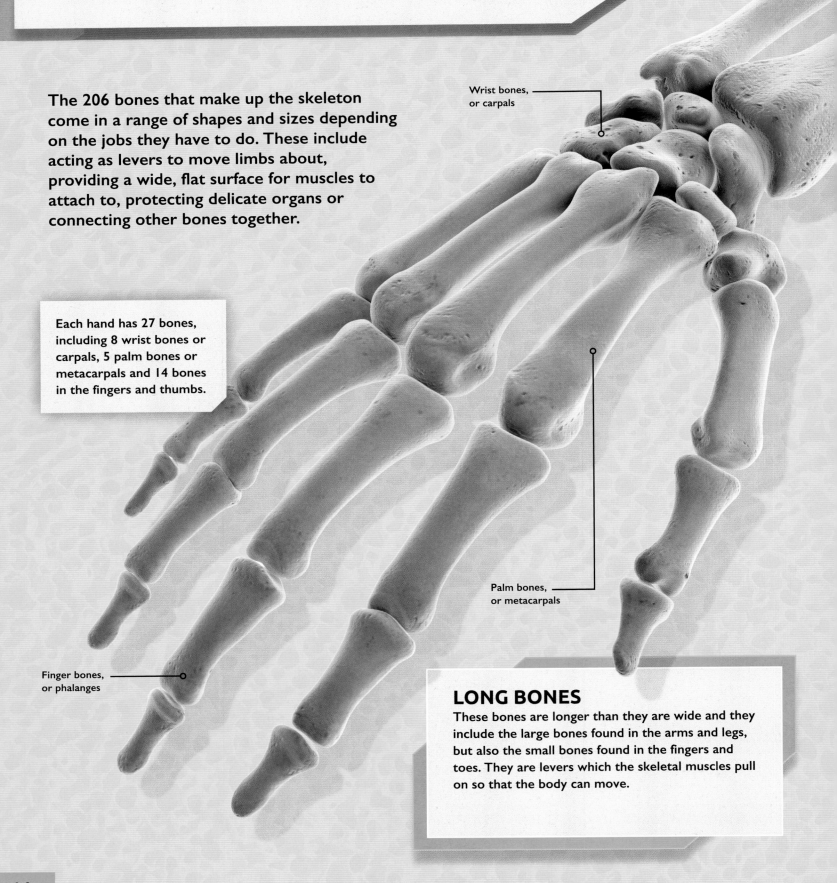

Wrist bones, or carpals

Each hand has 27 bones, including 8 wrist bones or carpals, 5 palm bones or metacarpals and 14 bones in the fingers and thumbs.

Palm bones, or metacarpals

Finger bones, or phalanges

LONG BONES
These bones are longer than they are wide and they include the large bones found in the arms and legs, but also the small bones found in the fingers and toes. They are levers which the skeletal muscles pull on so that the body can move.

SHORT BONES

These bones are usually as wide as they are long and they include the tarsals (found in the ankles) and the carpals (found in the wrists). They only provide a limited amount of movement and they act as a solid base for other bones.

FLAT BONES

These bones can be flat (as the name suggests), but they can also be curved or thin. They include the ribs, the breastbone (sternum), skull bones (cranium) and the shoulder blades (scapulae). Their flat shape means that they offer a large area for muscles to attach to, as with the shoulder blades (scapulae), or they protect a delicate body part underneath, as with the skull bones (cranium) protecting the brain.

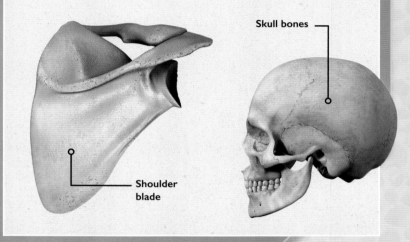

Skull bones

Shoulder blade

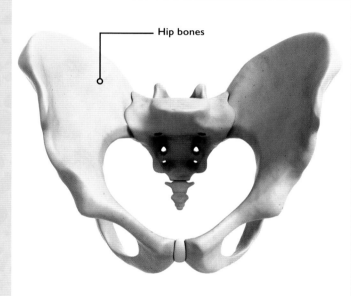

Hip bones

IRREGULAR BONES

These bones have no regular shape and do not fit into any of the other bone type. They perform a wide range of roles and include the hip bones, some of the bones in the face and the vertebrae that protect the spinal cord and act as attachments for the back muscles.

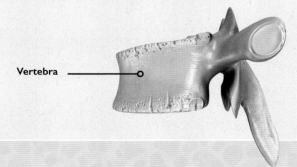

Vertebra

SESAMOID BONES

These bones are found inside some of the body's tendons, the cords that connect muscles to bones, and they include the kneecap (patella). They help to protect the tendon and improve how a joint works.

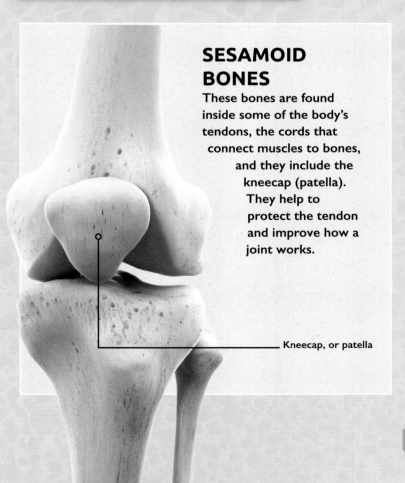

Kneecap, or patella

INSIDE BONES

Even though bones come in different shapes and sizes, they all have a similar structure inside. Surrounding the bone is a thin layer called the periosteum and beneath this is a layer of thick, dense compact bone tissue, which surrounds a layer of spongy bone. Some of the larger bones have a space in the middle filled with bone marrow.

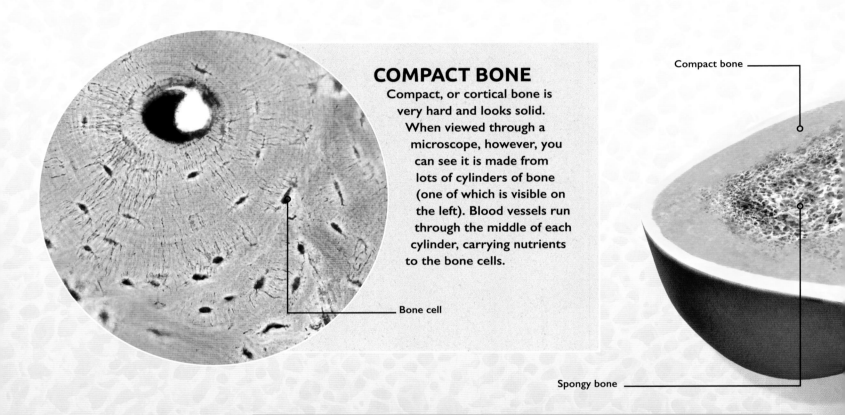

COMPACT BONE

Compact, or cortical bone is very hard and looks solid. When viewed through a microscope, however, you can see it is made from lots of cylinders of bone (one of which is visible on the left). Blood vessels run through the middle of each cylinder, carrying nutrients to the bone cells.

Bone cell

Compact bone

Spongy bone

SPONGY BONE

Spongy bone has lots of large spaces inside that make it look like a sponge. This lattice structure makes the bone very strong, and the gaps mean it is also very light. The spaces in spongy bone are often filled with bone marrow.

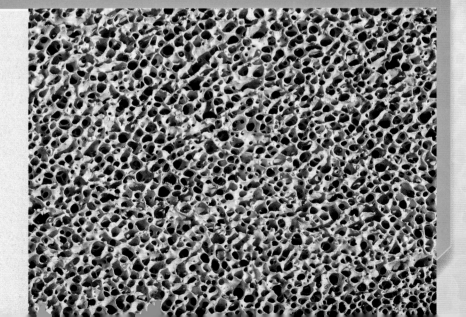

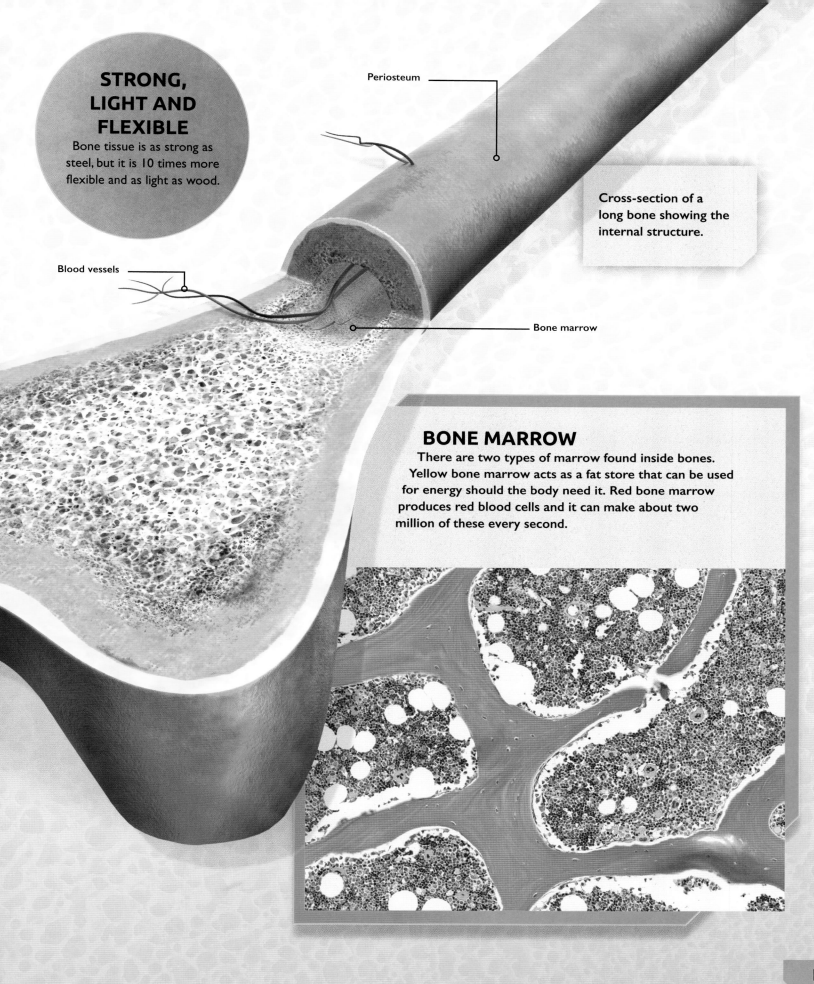

Periosteum

Cross-section of a long bone showing the internal structure.

Blood vessels

Bone marrow

BONE MARROW

There are two types of marrow found inside bones. Yellow bone marrow acts as a fat store that can be used for energy should the body need it. Red bone marrow produces red blood cells and it can make about two million of these every second.

BONE CELLS

The bones of a skeleton are always changing in response to different forces put upon the body. Bone cells deep inside the tissue are continually breaking it down and then reassembling it where it is needed the most.

OSTEOBLASTS

This type of bone cell is involved in growing parts of bones, by moving calcium from one part to another. These cells are usually found close to the surface of bones and in other areas where the bones are growing.

OSTEOCLASTS

These bone cells break down and absorb bone tissue where it is not needed. The components are then put back together to form new bone tissue where it is needed to repair the bone or to make it stronger. Osteoclasts are found in areas where the bone tissue is being reabsorbed and they are derived from monocytes, a type of white blood cell (see pages 58–59).

OSTEOCYTES

These are found in bones that are fully developed. They have a main body that sits inside a small opening in the bone tissue called a lacuna. Sprouting from this main body are thin strands that stretch out into the bone tissue along tiny tubes called canaliculi. Their job is to maintain the bone tissue.

Osteocyte

Osteoblasts

Osteoclasts

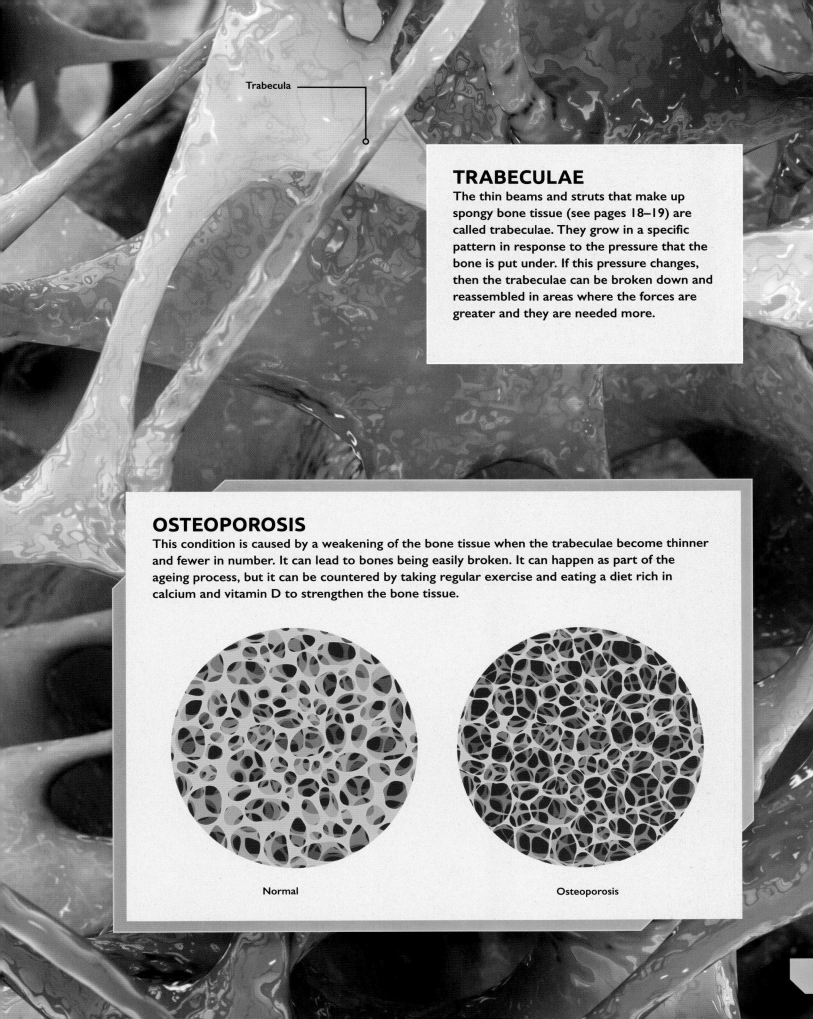

Trabecula

TRABECULAE

The thin beams and struts that make up spongy bone tissue (see pages 18–19) are called trabeculae. They grow in a specific pattern in response to the pressure that the bone is put under. If this pressure changes, then the trabeculae can be broken down and reassembled in areas where the forces are greater and they are needed more.

OSTEOPOROSIS

This condition is caused by a weakening of the bone tissue when the trabeculae become thinner and fewer in number. It can lead to bones being easily broken. It can happen as part of the ageing process, but it can be countered by taking regular exercise and eating a diet rich in calcium and vitamin D to strengthen the bone tissue.

Normal

Osteoporosis

GROWING BONES

Your bones will continue to grow throughout childhood and until you become an adult. They first appear inside the foetus in the womb and continue to grow until we are fully grown adults. Our bones usually stop growing around the age of 20, although they can become thicker after this age.

CARTILAGE

The bones that form inside a developing foetus are made of a substance called cartilage. This bendy material is also found in the nose and ears where it holds them in shape, while remaining flexible. Cartilage also lines some joints (see pages 28–29), where it helps to keep things moving smoothly. As the foetus develops, the bone cells turn bendy cartilage into hard bone tissue in a process called ossification.

The flexible cartilage bones in a foetus allow the internal organs to grow as it develops inside the womb.

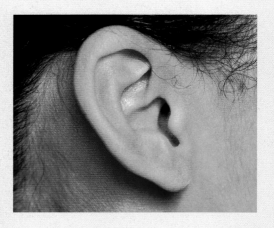

GROWING LONGER

An early long bone is made up of cartilage tissue. As it lengthens, a collar of bone tissue forms around the middle and blood vessels enter the bone to deliver nutrients. The blood vessels spread through the tissue and a central cavity forms for the marrow. After birth, blood vessels also enter the ends of the bone, called the epiphyses, and these become the main areas of bone growth.

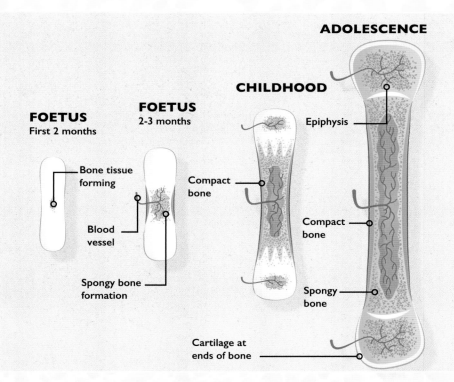

ADOLESCENCE

CHILDHOOD

FOETUS
First 2 months

FOETUS
2-3 months

Bone tissue forming

Blood vessel

Spongy bone formation

Compact bone

Epiphysis

Compact bone

Spongy bone

Cartilage at ends of bone

BABY BONES

When babies are born, they have around 300 bones in their bodies. Rather than the hard bones of a grown adult, these bones are still quite bendy. For example, the skull bones have yet to fuse together and have soft areas between them. These make the skull slightly flexible to help ease childbirth and also allow the skull to expand as the brain develops during the first weeks and months.

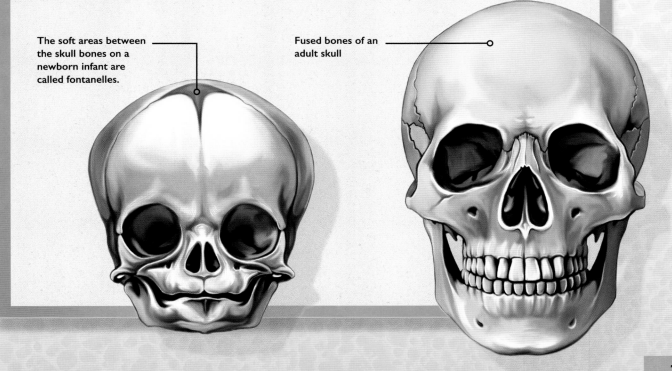

The soft areas between the skull bones on a newborn infant are called fontanelles.

Fused bones of an adult skull

REPAIRING BONES

Even though they are really strong, bones that are put under too much pressure can break, or fracture. However, as with most other body parts, bone tissue has the amazing ability to heal itself so that the bone is almost as good as new.

Doctors use X-ray images to spot and diagnose a broken bone.

HEALING TIME
Broken bones mend faster in children than in adults. A broken femur in a newborn infant will heal in just 3 weeks, but it could take 4–5 months for a broken femur to heal in an adult.

TYPES OF FRACTURE
There are different types of fracture depending on the complexity of the break and where it occurs:

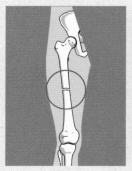 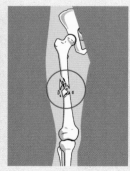 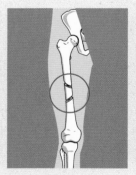 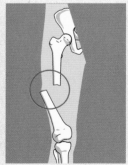 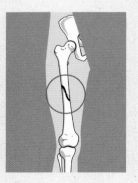

TRANSVERSE
When the bone has broken into two pieces at right angles to its length.

COMMINUTED
When the bone has broken into more than two pieces.

SEGMENTAL
When the bone has broken in at least two places, leaving a segment of bone totally separated.

COMPOUND
When the bone has broken and is poking through the skin's surface.

SPIRAL
When the bone has broken in a twisted pattern.

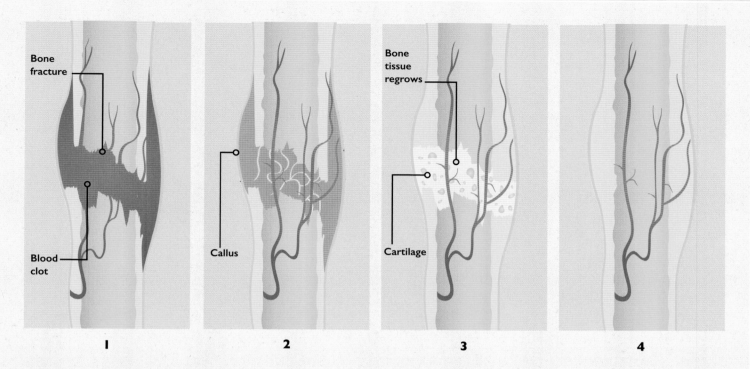

Bone
fracture

Blood
clot

Callus

Bone
tissue
regrows

Cartilage

1   2   3   4

THE STAGES OF HEALING

1 – A blood clot (see pages 120–121) forms around the fracture to prevent blood loss.

2 – After a few days a hard lump, or callus, forms over the fracture.

3 – Cartilage forms across the fracture, joining the broken ends of the bone, while bone cells produce bone tissue underneath.

4 – Blood vessels grow back across the fracture and bone tissue completely replaces the cartilage to repair the bone.

A HELPING HAND

To help bones heal correctly, doctors may wrap the body part in a hard cast to prevent movement. However, if the break is really bad and the bones aren't aligned properly, then doctors may have to use surgery to line them up and metal pins and plates to hold them in place while the broken bone knits itself back together.

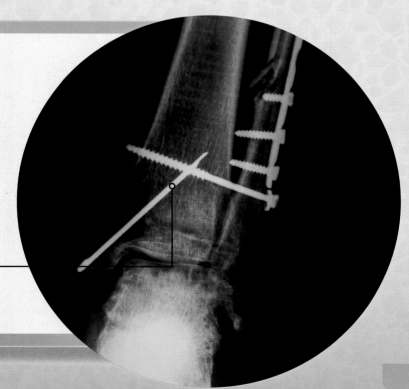

The pins, screws and plates that are visible in this X-ray are holding together these broken ankle bones as they heal.

WHERE BONES MEET

The places where two or more bones meet are known as joints. The human body has many different types of joint, whose shape depends on the job they have to do. These include joints that have little or no movement at all to those that can move a great to deal.

HYOID

The hyoid bone is found under your lower jaw and it is the only bone in the body that is not joined to another bone. Instead, it attaches to your tongue, giving it a base on which to move about.

Hyoid bone

RIGID JOINTS

In some cases, bones are fused together, creating rigid joints that don't move at all. Your skull is made up of 22 separate bones, but only one of these, the lower jaw, can move. The others are joined together at wiggly lines called sutures that hold them firmly in place. These bones provide the base for your facial features and also protect the fragile brain.

Suture joint

The lower jaw has the only movable joint in your skull

SLIGHTLY MOVEABLE JOINTS

Some joints feature bones that are held together by plates of cartilage or by discs. These joints will only move a little. However, if several of them work together, then their small motions can act together to produce quite a lot of movement, as in the vertebrae that make up the backbone.

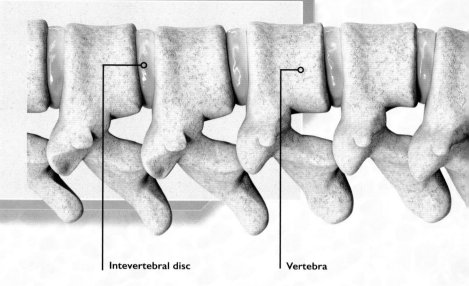

Intevertebral disc   Vertebra

POPPING JOINTS

Sometimes, your joints will pop and crack when you bend them. This sound is caused by gas being forced out of the fluid that is found inside the joint.

Always keep your back straight when lifting heavy objects

Regular exercise and stretching can improve the flexibilty of your joints.

KEEPING JOINTS HEALTHY

In order to keep your joints healthy, you should exercise regularly to improve muscle strength, posture and flexibility. A balanced diet will provide the nutrients you need to keep joints moving smoothly. It's also important to protect joints by lifting heavy objects correctly to reduce stress and wear.

FREELY MOVING JOINTS

The most well-known joints in the body are the ones that move the most. These freely moving joints are found in the arms and legs. These are known as synovial joints, after the synovial fluid that sits in between the bones and lubricates their movement.

Bone

Synovial membrane

Ligament

Synovial fluid

Cartilage

Where bones meet in a synovial joint, their surfaces are covered with smooth cartilage and the joint itself is surrounded by a capsule containing synovial fluid to aid movement.

HINGE JOINTS

This type of joint only allows movement in one plane, just like a door hinge. This means you can bend and straighten body parts, such as the elbows, knees, fingers and toes.

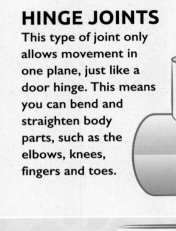

BALL-AND-SOCKET JOINTS

In these joints, the end of one bone is ball-shaped and sits inside the cup-shaped end of another bone. This joint type is found in the hips and shoulders and allows you to move your arms and legs in many different directions.

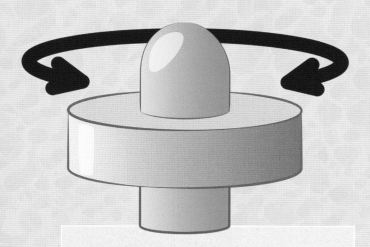

PIVOT JOINTS

This type of joint features a peg-shaped end of one bone that is surrounded by a ring of bone. It allows for side-to-side rotation and is found in the vertebrae in your neck.

CONDYLOID JOINTS

In these joints, also known as ellipsoidal joints, one bone has a dome-shaped end that sits in the shallow cup-shaped end of the other bone. Found in the knuckles and wrists, these joints allow for up and down and side-to-side movements.

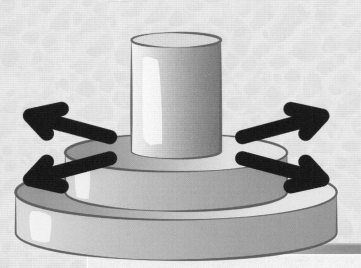

GLIDING JOINTS

These joints have flat surfaces that rub past each other a little. They are found where two bones fit together tightly, such as the bones that make up the foot.

SADDLE JOINTS

These joints have two concave or hollow surfaces that fit into each other and allow the bones to move side-to-side and back-and-forth. They are found in your thumbs and they help to make these digits more manoeuvrable than the fingers.

MUSCLE TISSUE

Your bones keep you in shape, but you need muscles to actually move around. And while you can control many of these muscles consciously, there are many more that are constantly at work without you being aware of them, helping to push things around your body to keep you alive.

Muscle fibre

Myofibril

Muscle filaments

HEAVY MUSCLES

In a fully grown human, the skeletal muscle tissue can make up as much as half of the total body weight.

MUSCLE TYPES

There are three different types of muscle tissue found in the human body:

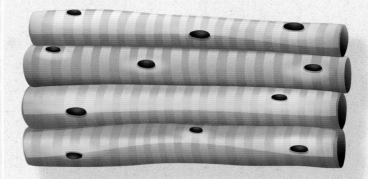

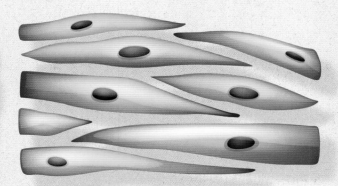

SKELETAL MUSCLE

This tissue forms the muscles that are attached to the bones of your skeleton and they move your limbs around. The fibres that make up this type of tissue are arranged in regular lines, giving it a striped, or striated, pattern.

SMOOTH MUSCLE

This muscle tissue is found in body organs, such as the stomach wall, and usually acts without you being aware of it. The muscle fibres are arranged irregularly, giving it a smooth appearance.

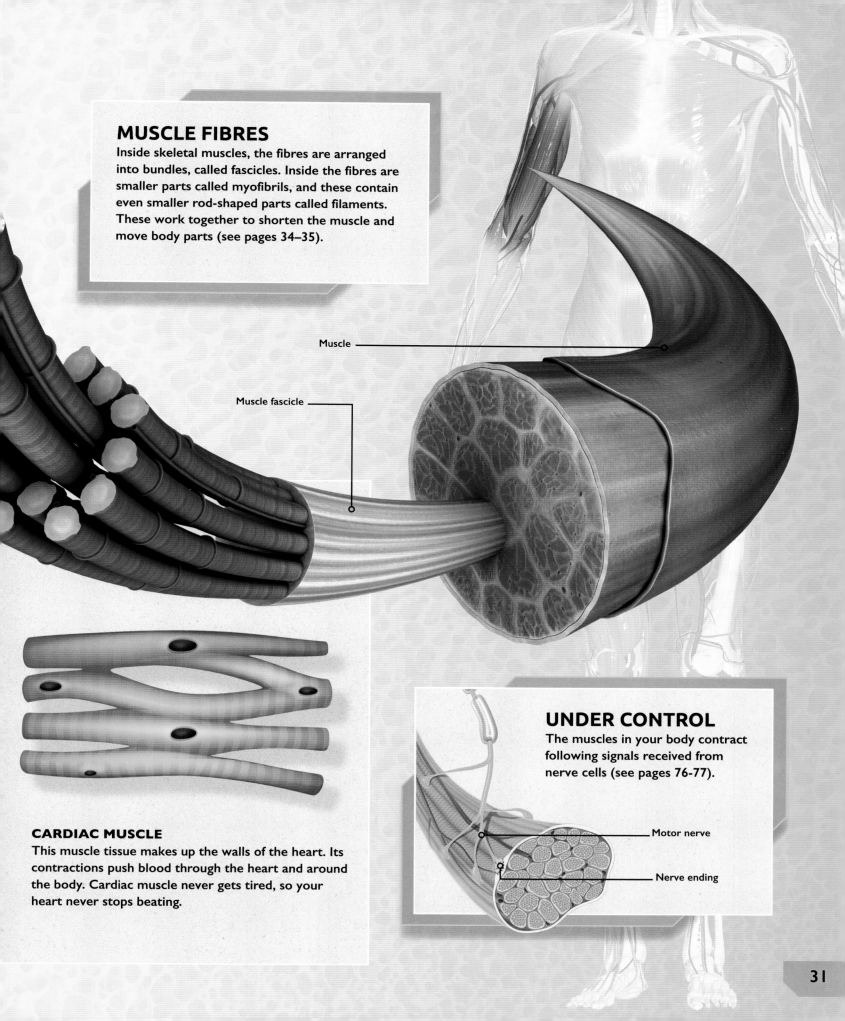

MUSCLE FIBRES

Inside skeletal muscles, the fibres are arranged into bundles, called fascicles. Inside the fibres are smaller parts called myofibrils, and these contain even smaller rod-shaped parts called filaments. These work together to shorten the muscle and move body parts (see pages 34–35).

Muscle

Muscle fascicle

CARDIAC MUSCLE

This muscle tissue makes up the walls of the heart. Its contractions push blood through the heart and around the body. Cardiac muscle never gets tired, so your heart never stops beating.

UNDER CONTROL

The muscles in your body contract following signals received from nerve cells (see pages 76-77).

Motor nerve

Nerve ending

SKELETAL MUSCLES

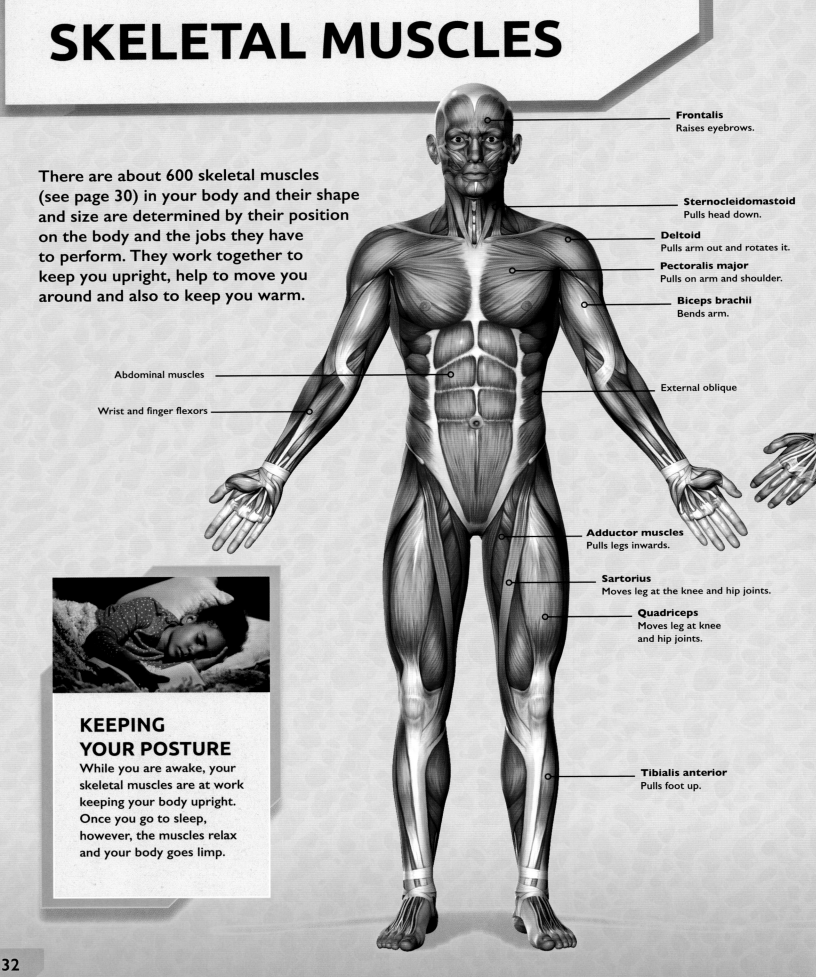

There are about 600 skeletal muscles (see page 30) in your body and their shape and size are determined by their position on the body and the jobs they have to perform. They work together to keep you upright, help to move you around and also to keep you warm.

Frontalis
Raises eyebrows.

Sternocleidomastoid
Pulls head down.

Deltoid
Pulls arm out and rotates it.

Pectoralis major
Pulls on arm and shoulder.

Biceps brachii
Bends arm.

Abdominal muscles

Wrist and finger flexors

External oblique

Adductor muscles
Pulls legs inwards.

Sartorius
Moves leg at the knee and hip joints.

Quadriceps
Moves leg at knee and hip joints.

Tibialis anterior
Pulls foot up.

KEEPING YOUR POSTURE

While you are awake, your skeletal muscles are at work keeping your body upright. Once you go to sleep, however, the muscles relax and your body goes limp.

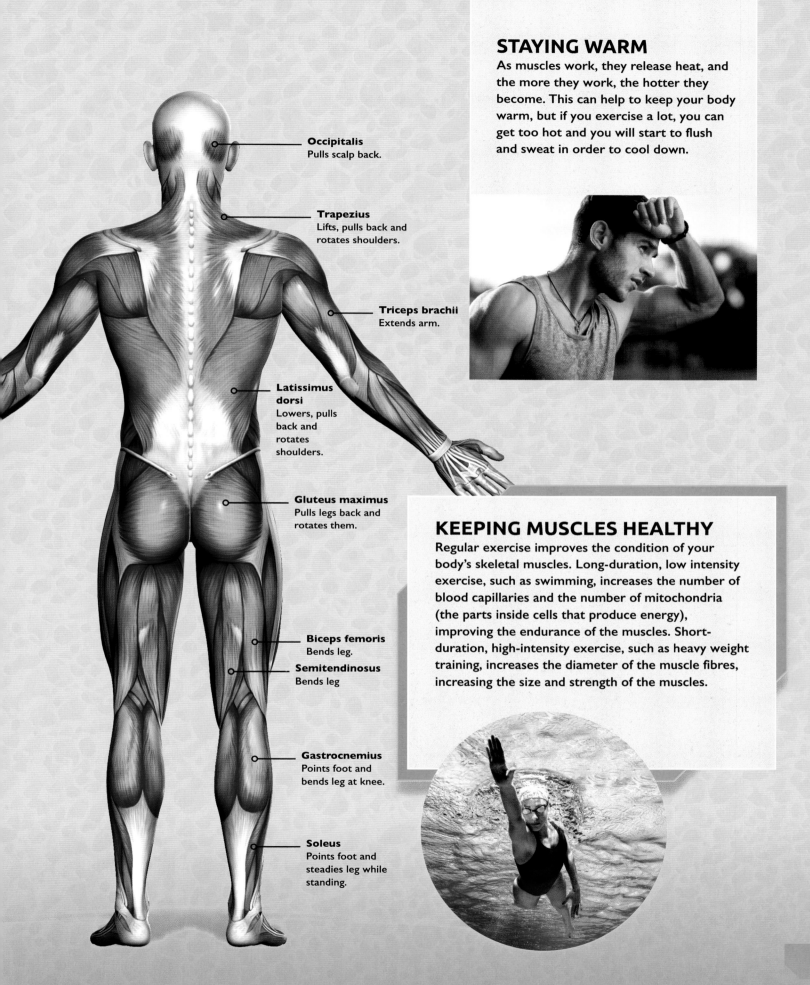

Occipitalis
Pulls scalp back.

Trapezius
Lifts, pulls back and rotates shoulders.

Triceps brachii
Extends arm.

Latissimus dorsi
Lowers, pulls back and rotates shoulders.

Gluteus maximus
Pulls legs back and rotates them.

Biceps femoris
Bends leg.

Semitendinosus
Bends leg

Gastrocnemius
Points foot and bends leg at knee.

Soleus
Points foot and steadies leg while standing.

STAYING WARM
As muscles work, they release heat, and the more they work, the hotter they become. This can help to keep your body warm, but if you exercise a lot, you can get too hot and you will start to flush and sweat in order to cool down.

KEEPING MUSCLES HEALTHY
Regular exercise improves the condition of your body's skeletal muscles. Long-duration, low intensity exercise, such as swimming, increases the number of blood capillaries and the number of mitochondria (the parts inside cells that produce energy), improving the endurance of the muscles. Short-duration, high-intensity exercise, such as heavy weight training, increases the diameter of the muscle fibres, increasing the size and strength of the muscles.

MOVING BODY PARTS

Muscle tissue is designed to one thing: pull. Working together in teams, the skeletal muscles around your body produce large motions, including bending arms, straightening legs and moving you from one place to another. They also perform many fine and delicate movements.

PULLING TOGETHER

When a nerve signal reaches a muscle with a command to get shorter, or contract, the muscle filaments slide together so that the muscle contracts. As it does so, it pulls on the bones it is attached to, making them move.

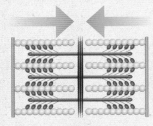
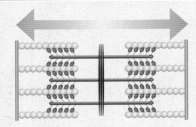

Contracting
Filaments slide together

Relaxing
Filaments slide apart

LEVERS IN THE BODY

Skeletal muscles move body parts by using a system of levers where a force is applied to move a load around a pivot, or fulcrum. The force is exerted by the muscle, the load involves the body part (and anything that may be held or attached), and the fulcrum is the movable joint. There are three different types of lever, and they can all be found around the body.

FIRST CLASS LEVERS

The fulcrum in a first class lever sits between the force and the load, as found in the base of the neck to move the head up and down.

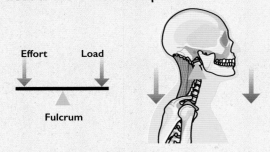

Effort   Load

Fulcrum

SECOND CLASS LEVERS

In a second class lever, the load sits between the force and the fulcrum, as found in the feet and calves.

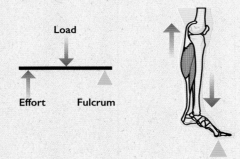

Load

Effort   Fulcrum

THIRD CLASS LEVERS

In this lever, the force is applied between the load and the fulcrum, as in the elbow and forearm.

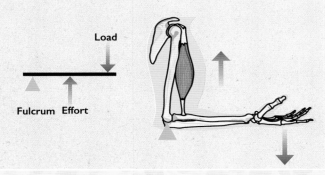

Load

Fulcrum Effort

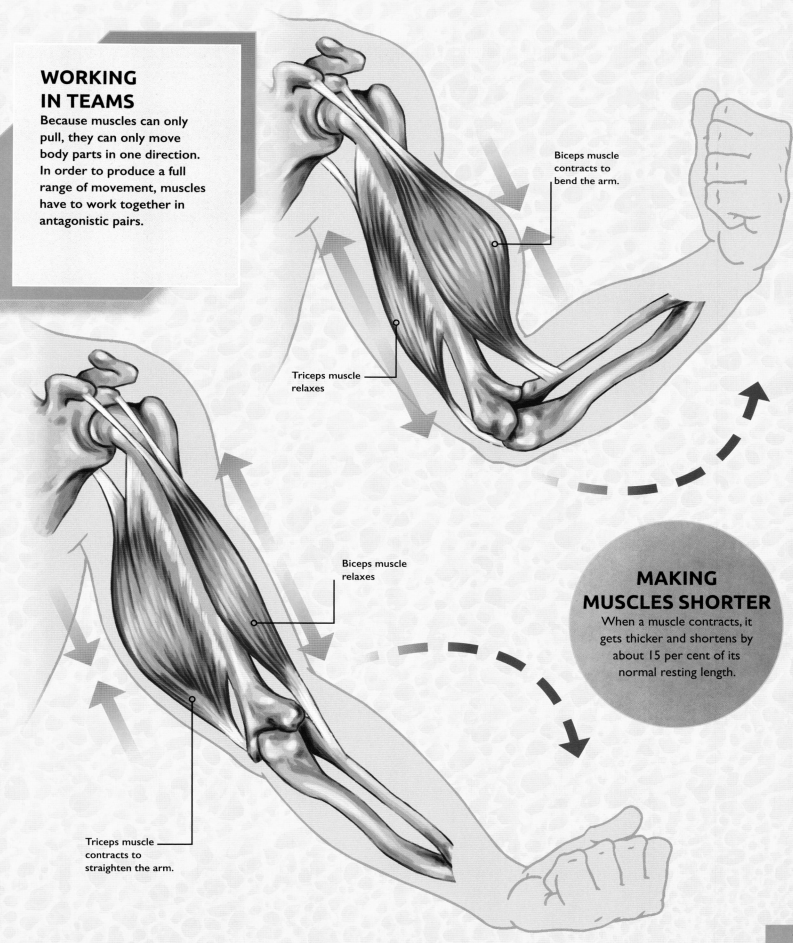

WORKING IN TEAMS

Because muscles can only pull, they can only move body parts in one direction. In order to produce a full range of movement, muscles have to work together in antagonistic pairs.

Biceps muscle contracts to bend the arm.

Triceps muscle relaxes

Biceps muscle relaxes

Triceps muscle contracts to straighten the arm.

MAKING MUSCLES SHORTER

When a muscle contracts, it gets thicker and shortens by about 15 per cent of its normal resting length.

FINE CONTROL

While some of the skeletal muscles are large and strong, there are many other small muscles that control every tiny action. These are most obvious in facial expressions such as blinking and frowning, but are also used in actions like holding a pen or moving your fingers.

FACIAL MUSCLES

The muscles that sit under the skin of your face (as well as a few in your scalp and neck) are responsible for pulling more than 7,000 facial expressions that show people how you are feeling.

EMOTIONS

The facial muscles pull on the skin, moving it around to produce facial expressions and communicate your emotions to others. For example, when you are happy, the muscles around your mouth pull the corners of the upper lip up to form a smile.

Happy
Muscles in the cheeks and above the mouth pull the lips up and apart to form a smile.

Angry
Muscles pull the eyebrows down and close the eyes slightly. Muscles around the mouth purse the lips.

Sad
Muscles below the mouth pull the lips down, forming a sad face.

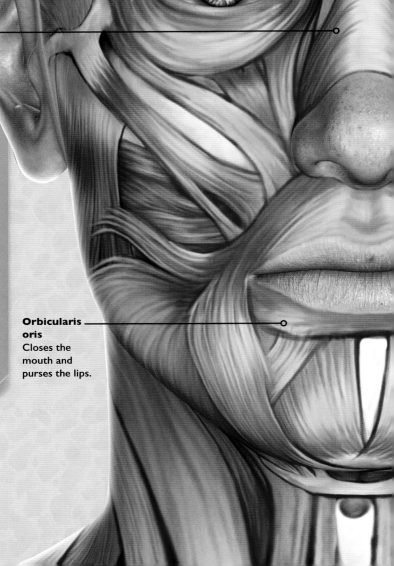

Frontalis
Raises eyebrows and wrinkles forehead.

Temporalis
Pulls the lower jaw up and back.

Procerus
Pulls eyebrows down and together.

Nasalis
Widens nasal openings.

Orbicularis oris
Closes the mouth and purses the lips.

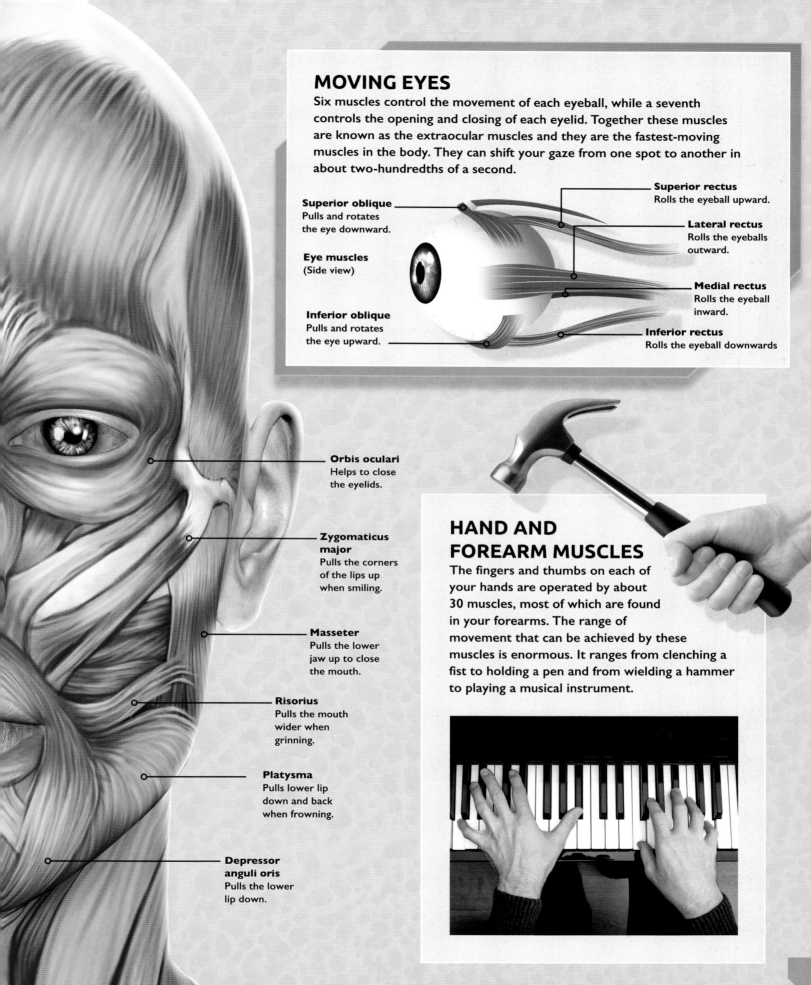

MOVING EYES

Six muscles control the movement of each eyeball, while a seventh controls the opening and closing of each eyelid. Together these muscles are known as the extraocular muscles and they are the fastest-moving muscles in the body. They can shift your gaze from one spot to another in about two-hundredths of a second.

Superior oblique
Pulls and rotates the eye downward.

Eye muscles
(Side view)

Inferior oblique
Pulls and rotates the eye upward.

Superior rectus
Rolls the eyeball upward.

Lateral rectus
Rolls the eyeballs outward.

Medial rectus
Rolls the eyeball inward.

Inferior rectus
Rolls the eyeball downwards

Orbis oculari
Helps to close the eyelids.

Zygomaticus major
Pulls the corners of the lips up when smiling.

Masseter
Pulls the lower jaw up to close the mouth.

Risorius
Pulls the mouth wider when grinning.

Platysma
Pulls lower lip down and back when frowning.

Depressor anguli oris
Pulls the lower lip down.

HAND AND FOREARM MUSCLES

The fingers and thumbs on each of your hands are operated by about 30 muscles, most of which are found in your forearms. The range of movement that can be achieved by these muscles is enormous. It ranges from clenching a fist to holding a pen and from wielding a hammer to playing a musical instrument.

TENDONS AND LIGAMENTS

Muscles cannot act on their own – they need tendons to connect to body parts so they can pull on the skeleton and skin. And joints would fall apart if they didn't have tough ligaments to hold them together.

LIGAMENTS

Holding many of the joints together are thick, strong straps, called ligaments. These allow the bones to move in certain directions, but stop them from falling apart from each other. However, a strong blow or twist can pull the bones out of line, or dislocate the joint. When this happens, the bones have to be pushed back into place so that they line up correctly.

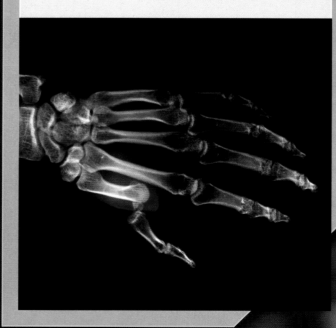

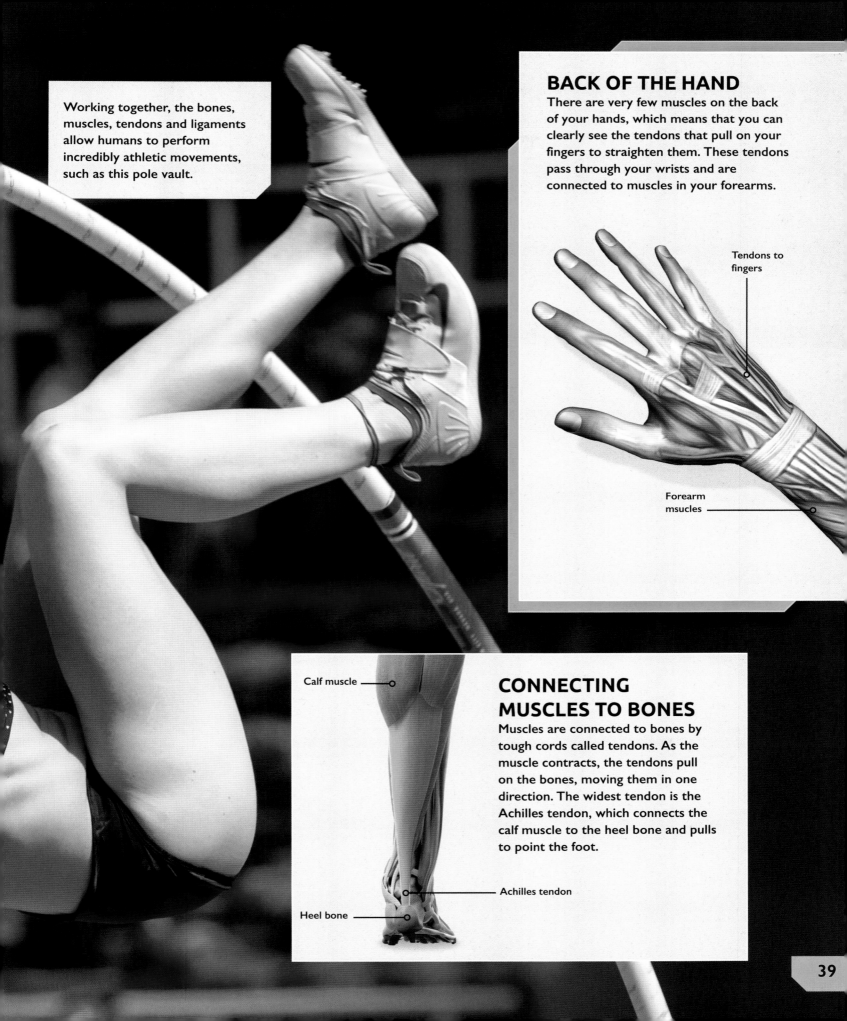

Working together, the bones, muscles, tendons and ligaments allow humans to perform incredibly athletic movements, such as this pole vault.

BACK OF THE HAND

There are very few muscles on the back of your hands, which means that you can clearly see the tendons that pull on your fingers to straighten them. These tendons pass through your wrists and are connected to muscles in your forearms.

Tendons to fingers

Forearm msucles

Calf muscle

CONNECTING MUSCLES TO BONES

Muscles are connected to bones by tough cords called tendons. As the muscle contracts, the tendons pull on the bones, moving them in one direction. The widest tendon is the Achilles tendon, which connects the calf muscle to the heel bone and pulls to point the foot.

Achilles tendon

Heel bone

SUPPLYING THE BODY
DIGESTION AND BREATHING

In order to keep your body healthy and fit, it needs a regular intake of nutrients. These come from the food you eat.

When food enters your body, it starts a journey down a long tube called the digestive system, which begins with your mouth and ends with your anus. As it passes through this tube, the food is broken down, physically and chemically, into smaller and smaller pieces, until the pieces are small enough to pass through the walls of the intestine and into your blood.

From there, these nutrients are carried to every part of your body and delivered to every cell, where they are used to produce energy and the raw materials to build new cells and repair damaged ones.

In order to release energy from some of the nutrients, however, your body also needs a supply of oxygen. It obtains this from the air, by breathing it into two large inflatable sacs, called the lungs, which are inside your chest. Inside the lungs, oxygen passes into the bloodstream, while waste carbon dioxide passes the other way so that it can be breathed out of the body.

A healthy diet should contain all the nutrients your body needs to stay fit and well, including carbohydrates, proteins, fats, minerals and vitamins. However, too much of certain foods can be bad for your body and cause lasting damage.

A HEALTHY DIET

In order to keep your body fit and healthy, it's important that you eat the right food types and that you eat a balanced diet. This will give your body the energy to carry out your daily functions and the raw materials it needs to build and repair itself.

ENERGY LEVELS

The amount of energy that foods can offer is measured in kilojoules or kilocalories. How much energy you need throughout the day depends on how old you are and what you do.

APPROXIMATE ENERGY NEEDS		
Age	**Male**	**Female**
2–3	1,088 kcal/day	1,004 kcal/day
4–6	1,482 kcal/day	1,378 kcal/day
7–10	1,817 kcal/day	1,703 kcal/day
11–64	2,500 kcal/day	2,000 kcal/day
65–74	2,342 kcal/day	1,912 kcal/day
75+	2,294 kcal/day	1,840 kcal/day

MINERALS
Your body needs a wide range of minerals to carry out different jobs in the body. For example, it needs calcium to keep your bones strong, iron to make red blood cells and potassium to keep your muscles, heart and nervous system working properly.

CARBOHYDRATES
These provide your body with energy and they should form the largest part of your diet. They are found in foods that are rich in starch and sugars, such as potatoes, rice and pasta. However, if you eat too many carbohydrates, your body converts them into fats, which it stores in the adipose (fatty) tissue just below the surface of your skin.

FATS

Fats can be found in solid foods, such as meat or cheese, or in liquids, including cooking oils. Fats are an essential part of your diet as they supply your body with energy and are used to support cell growth, protect organs and absorb vital nutrients. Fat contains lots of energy, meaning it's high in calories.

WATER

Your body is about 60 per cent water, which helps it in a great many ways, including maintaining normal body temperature, keeping joints lubricated, protecting sensitive tissues and getting rid of waste. How much water you need depends on how active you are and where you live – an active person needs to drink a lot of water as does someone who lives in a warm climate.

PROTEINS

These are used by your body to repair cells and grow new tissue. Foods that are rich in protein include meat and fish, dairy products and nuts, as well as pulses, such as beans, lentils and chickpeas.

FIBRE

Roughage, or fibre, doesn't supply your body with nutrients, but it provides a solid mass for the intestine muscles to push against. A lack of fibre can lead to digestive problems, such as constipation. Foods that are high in fibre include grains, fruit (with skin) and pulses.

VITAMINS

Vitamins are complex chemicals that your body needs to perform certain tasks. They are named using different letters. For example, ascorbic acid (vitamin C), is found in citrus fruits. It is used by the body to build blood vessels, muscles, cartilage and collagen in bones and to repair damage. A lack of vitamin C can lead to a condition called scurvy, which can lead to the swelling of body parts, bleeding, teeth loss, joint pain and, if left untreated, death.

THE DIGESTIVE SYSTEM

In order to get the nutrients your body requires, the food you eat has to be broken down into smaller pieces that can be absorbed. This process is called digestion and it occurs as your food takes its long trip along the digestive system.

DIGESTION

Different types of food are broken down, or digested, into smaller parts as they pass through the intestines.

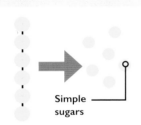

CARBOHYDRATES
These are split up into simple sugars. For example, starch is a complex carbohydrate that is broken down into simple sugars, such as glucose.

Simple sugars

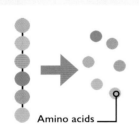

PROTEINS
These are broken down into simple amino acids.

Amino acids

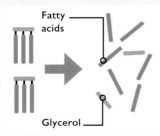

Fatty acids

FATS
These are broken down to glycerol and fatty acids.

Glycerol

ENZYMES

The digestion of food is sped up by special chemicals called enzymes, which are produced by different organs along the digestive tract. Your body produces lots of different enzymes as each type of food needs a specific enzyme to break it down. For example, salivary amylase, found in saliva, starts the breakdown of starch into simpler molecules.

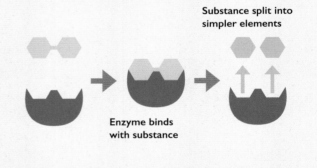

Substance split into simpler elements

Enzyme binds with substance

LONG JOURNEY
Measured from one end to the other, the digestive system of an adult human can be up to 9 m (30 ft) long.

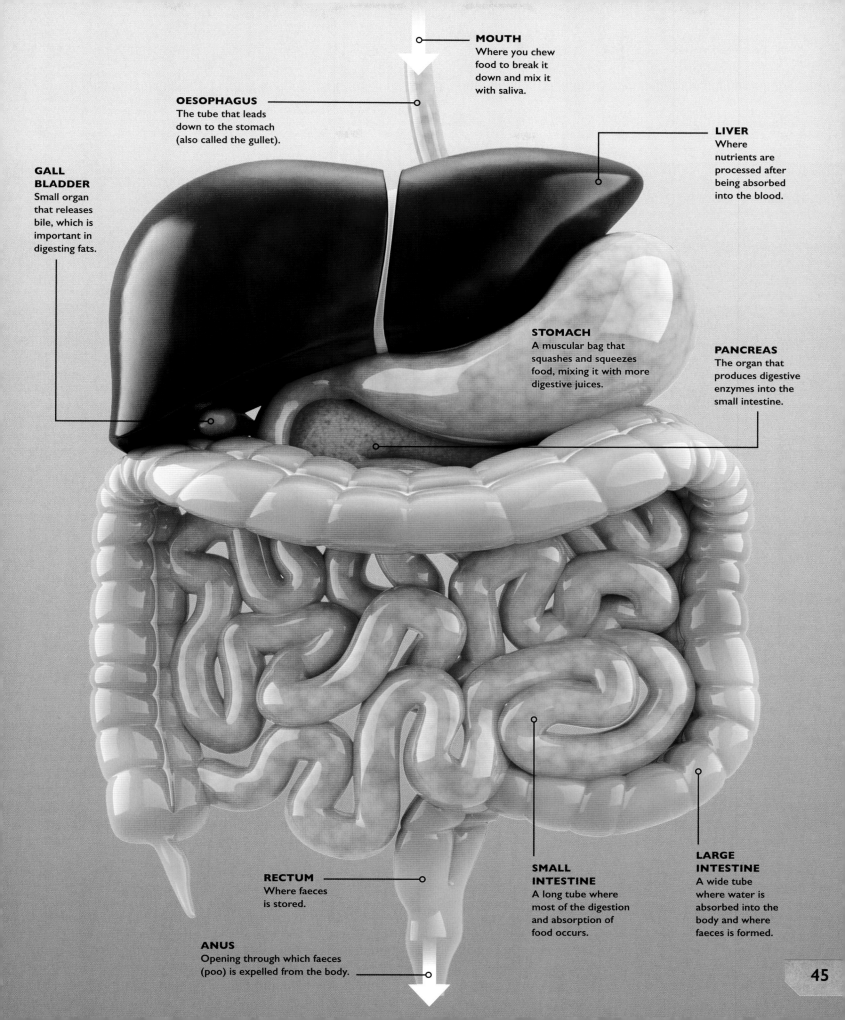

MOUTH
Where you chew food to break it down and mix it with saliva.

OESOPHAGUS
The tube that leads down to the stomach (also called the gullet).

LIVER
Where nutrients are processed after being absorbed into the blood.

GALL BLADDER
Small organ that releases bile, which is important in digesting fats.

STOMACH
A muscular bag that squashes and squeezes food, mixing it with more digestive juices.

PANCREAS
The organ that produces digestive enzymes into the small intestine.

RECTUM
Where faeces is stored.

SMALL INTESTINE
A long tube where most of the digestion and absorption of food occurs.

LARGE INTESTINE
A wide tube where water is absorbed into the body and where faeces is formed.

ANUS
Opening through which faeces (poo) is expelled from the body.

THE MOUTH

Food begins its journey
in the mouth where it is
squashed and chewed and
mixed with saliva to make
it soft enough to swallow
and travel down into
the stomach.

SALIVA

This liquid is produced by
three pairs of glands located
around the mouth. It helps
to turn the food soft so that
it can be swallowed and it
contains an enzyme called
salivary amylase, which starts
the digestion process.

Nasal
cavity

Uvula

Teeth

Lips

Jaw

Tongue

Pharynx

Epiglottis

LIPS AND
TONGUE

The lips form the opening
to the mouth and muscles
that control them help to guide
food towards the teeth for chewing.
Once inside the mouth, the muscly tongue helps to
move food around the mouth, pushing it to form a
squashed ball of mushy food called a bolus. Once the
food has been chewed, the tongue then pushes it to
the top of the throat, or pharynx, for swallowing.
The tongue is also covered in thousands of taste
buds, which tell you what flavour your food is (see
pages 98–99).

Larynx

Trachea

Oesophagus

TEETH

Throughout your life, you will have two sets of teeth – the baby or milk teeth that come through not long after birth and the adult teeth. An adult has 32 teeth with different shapes for different jobs.

INCISORS
These chisel-shaped teeth at the front of the mouth bite and tear food into small chunks.

CANINES
These pointed teeth help to grasp and hold food.

PREMOLARS AND MOLARS
These large teeth squash and break down food while chewing.

INSIDE TEETH

Teeth need to be tough to cope with lots of biting and chewing every day. They also need a supply of blood to keep them healthy and alive.

Crown
This is covered with enamel – the hardest substance in the body.

Dentine
Under the enamel is a layer of dentine which makes up most of the tooth.

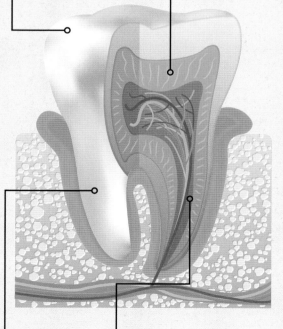

Root
This is fixed into the bone of the jaw.

Pulp
At the centre of the tooth is the pulp, which contains the nerve endings and blood vessels.

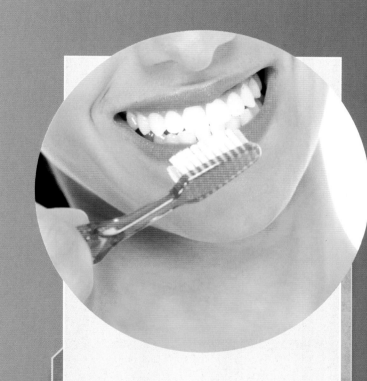

KEEPING TEETH HEALTHY

Enamel may be the hardest substance in the body, but it still needs to be looked after if it is to last your whole life. If teeth aren't cleaned regularly, then food can build up on them, attracting bacteria, which release substances that can eat away at the enamel, producing holes, or cavities.

INTO THE STOMACH

After the mouth, the stomach is the next part of the digestive process. Chewed food is pushed to the back of the mouth and swallowed. It passes down the oesophagus and into the stomach for the next stage in digestion.

PERISTALSIS

Food is pushed along by waves of muscle contractions in the intestine walls. This is called peristalsis and it is why we can eat while standing on our heads and astronauts can eat in space without gravity!

SWALLOWING

As well as the opening to the oesophagus, the back of the mouth has openings to the nasal passages above and the windpipe, or trachea, which leads to the lungs. It is very important that food doesn't make its way into these openings, especially the trachea, where it can cause choking. The soft palate at the back of the roof of the mouth stops food moving up into the nasal passages. Beneath the tongue at the back of the throat is a flap called the epiglottis, which closes the opening to the trachea as food is swallowed.

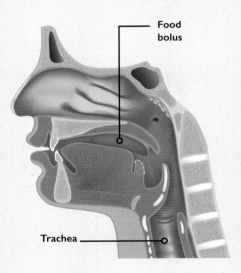

Food bolus

Trachea

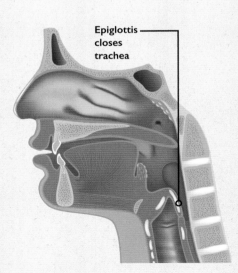

Epiglottis closes trachea

IN THE STOMACH

The inside walls of the stomach are lined with lots of little pits that release gastric juices. These juices contain hydrochloric acid. This kills unwanted germs and bacteria that may be present in the food. It also contains enzymes, such as pepsin, which helps to break down proteins, and lipase, which helps to break down fats.

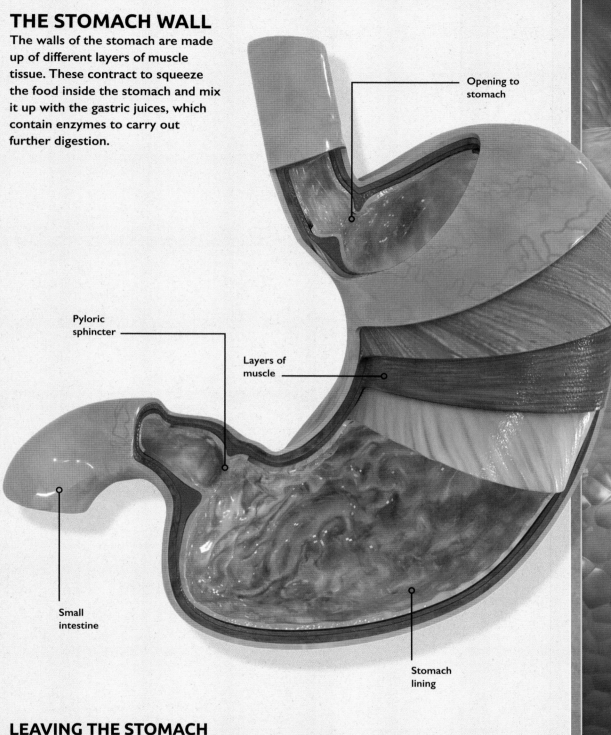

THE STOMACH WALL

The walls of the stomach are made up of different layers of muscle tissue. These contract to squeeze the food inside the stomach and mix it up with the gastric juices, which contain enzymes to carry out further digestion.

Opening to stomach

Pyloric sphincter

Layers of muscle

Small intestine

Stomach lining

LEAVING THE STOMACH

After between one and three hours inside the stomach, food has been squashed and squeezed to form a runny substance called chyme. A ring of muscle called the pyloric sphincter, which forms the exit from the stomach, opens a little and the stomach walls contract to push the chyme out into the small intestine.

THE SMALL INTESTINE

The next part of the digestive system is the small intestine. It is the longest part of your gut, measuring in at more than 6 m (20 ft) long. Fortunately, this mammoth tube is coiled up into the small area just below your stomach.

LONG JOURNEY

It can take food between 24 and 72 hours to complete its trip through the entire digestive system.

PARTS OF THE SMALL INTESTINE

The small intestine is divided up into three parts. The first part, the duodenum, is the shortest at around 25 cm (10 in) in length. It receives the chyme from the stomach and digestive juices from the gall bladder and the pancreas (see pages 52–53). The second part of the small intestine is the jejunum, which is about 2.5 m (8 ft) long. The final section is the ileum, which is about 3.5 m (12 ft) long. Most of the absorption of food takes place in the jejunum and ileum.

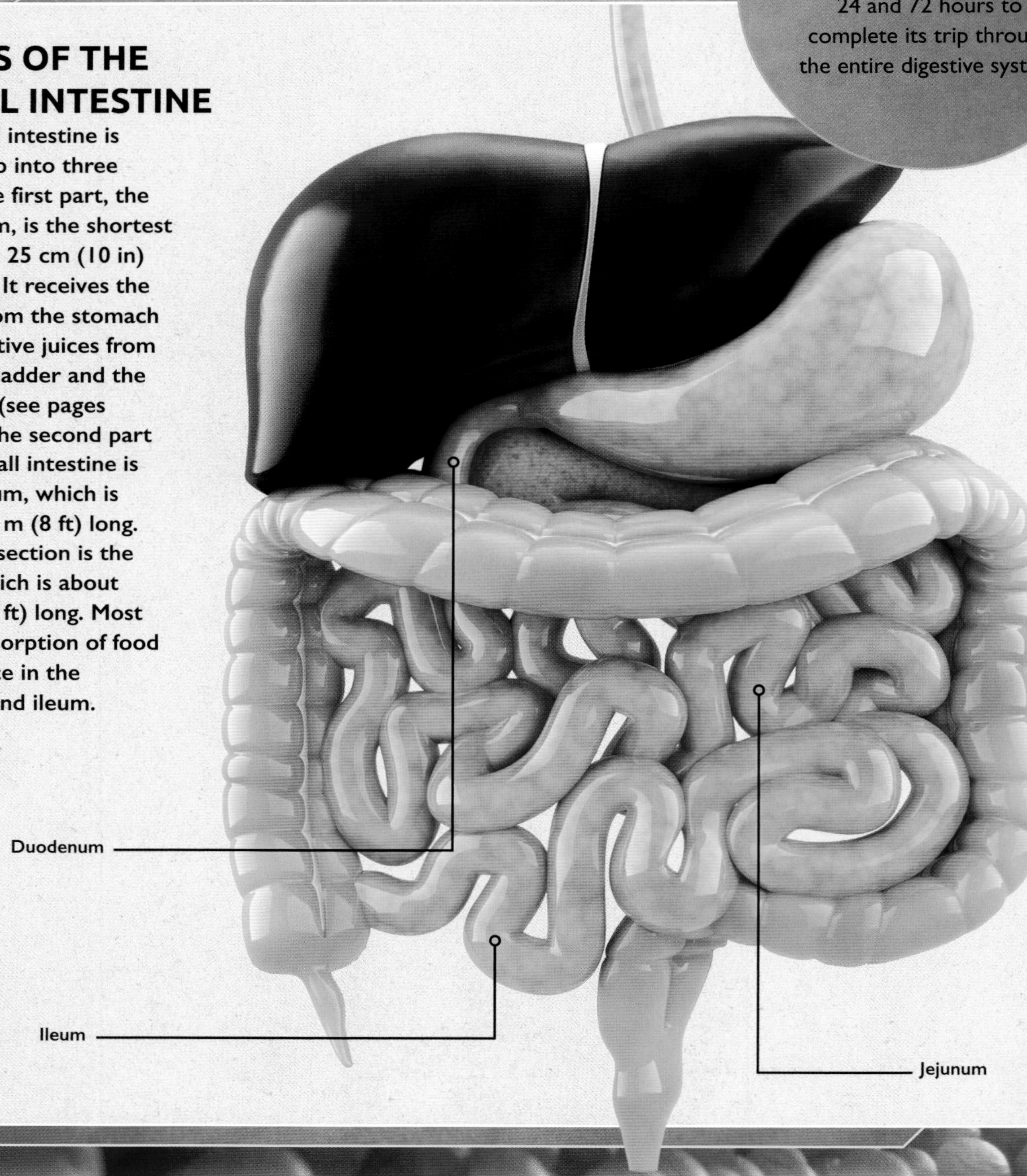

Duodenum

Ileum

Jejunum

INTESTINE WALLS

The walls of the small intestine have layers of muscle which squeeze to push the chyme along and mix it up. The surfaces of the walls are covered with millions of tiny finger-like structures called villi (main image). These greatly increase the surface area of the small intestine, helping with the absorption of nutrients.

FURTHER DIGESTION

Although the small intestine doesn't release any enzymes itself, it is the site of further digestion. Proteins are broken up into amino acids, while the enzymes sucrase, maltase and lactase break down carbohydrates into simple sugars.

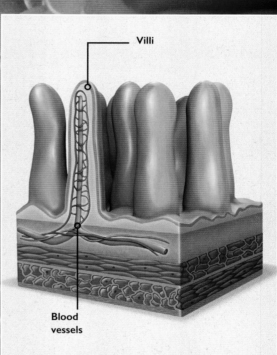

Villi

Blood vessels

ABSORBING FOOD

Inside villi are tiny blood vessels called capillaries. Digested food molecules, such as amino acids and glucose, can pass through the walls of the villi and into the blood to be carried around the body. Fatty acids are absorbed into lymph capillaries (see pages 120–121) and they are carried to the liver for processing (see pages 52–53).

THE LIVER, GALL BLADDER AND PANCREAS

Both the gall bladder and the pancreas release vital digestive enzymes that play key roles in breaking down food in the small intestine. The liver is a wedge-shaped organ that is located just beneath the diaphragm. It is the body's chemical processing plant, carrying out hundreds of different jobs, including processing nutrients from the food you eat.

Diaphragm

Right lobe of the liver

PANCREAS

The pancreas is about 12–15 cm (4.5–6 inches) long and is tucked just beneath the stomach. It produces about 1.5 l (2.5 pints) of pancreatic juices every day, which empty into the small intestine. These juices include chemicals that help enzymes work as well as enzymes that break down fats and carbohydrates. The pancreas also releases hormones that control the levels of sugar in the blood (see pages 110–111).

GALL BLADDER

The gall bladder is a small pear-shaped organ that stores and releases a chemical called bile into the small intestine and this plays a key role in breaking down fats. Bile also contains bile pigments, which are made from breaking down old and worn-out red blood cells. Bile pigments give faeces its colour.

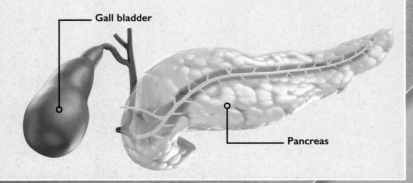

Gall bladder

Pancreas

Gall bladder

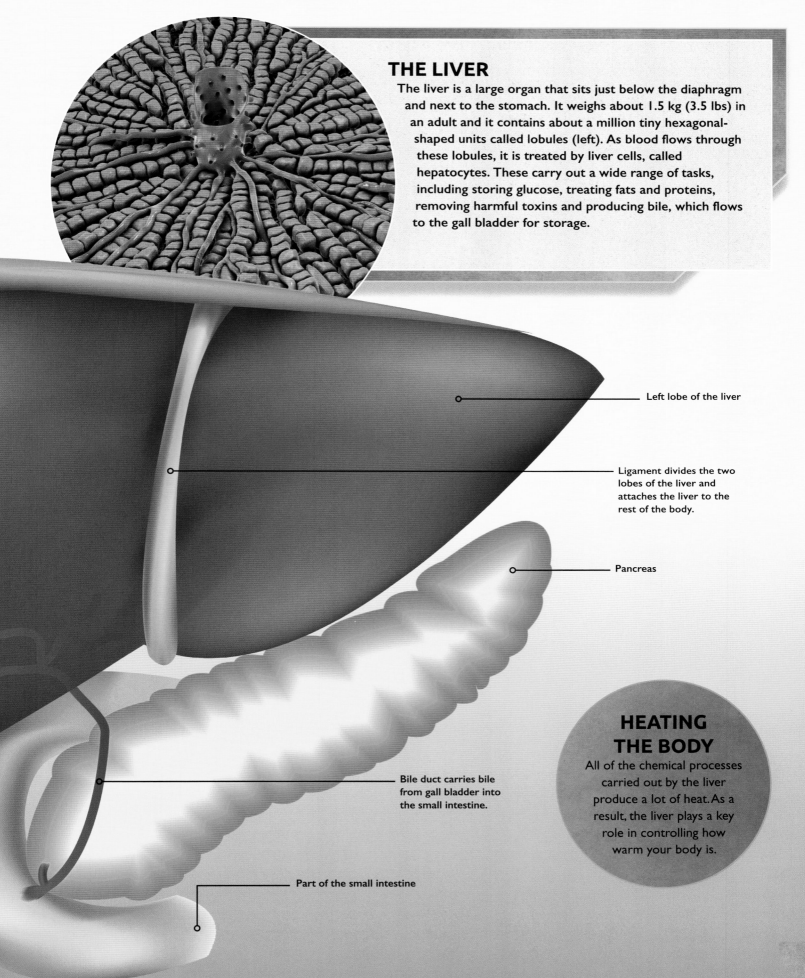

THE LIVER

The liver is a large organ that sits just below the diaphragm and next to the stomach. It weighs about 1.5 kg (3.5 lbs) in an adult and it contains about a million tiny hexagonal-shaped units called lobules (left). As blood flows through these lobules, it is treated by liver cells, called hepatocytes. These carry out a wide range of tasks, including storing glucose, treating fats and proteins, removing harmful toxins and producing bile, which flows to the gall bladder for storage.

Left lobe of the liver

Ligament divides the two lobes of the liver and attaches the liver to the rest of the body.

Pancreas

Bile duct carries bile from gall bladder into the small intestine.

Part of the small intestine

HEATING THE BODY

All of the chemical processes carried out by the liver produce a lot of heat. As a result, the liver plays a key role in controlling how warm your body is.

THE LARGE INTESTINE

Running around the tightly coiled small intestine is the final part of the digestive system – the large intestine. This receives the unwanted parts of the food you eat, absorbs much of the water from it and turns what's left into faeces that's pushed out of your body when you go to the toilet.

Transverse colon

Ascending colon

Caecum

Appendix

Descending colon

Rectum

Anus

PARTS OF THE LARGE INTESTINE

The last part of the small intestine, the ileum, empties in the caecum, which is a small pouch about 6 cm (2.5 in) long. Hanging off to one side of the caecum is the small, finger-like appendix. Rising up from the caecum, the colon has three parts – the ascending, transverse and descending colon, which run around the small intestine. At the end of the large intestine are the rectum and the anus.

THE APPENDIX

The appendix is the narrowest part of the digestive system and is between 5–15 cm (2–6 in) long. It can become blocked with bacteria and undigested food and this can cause it to swell and become sore – a condition known as appendicitis. In extreme cases, it can even burst, which can be very dangerous. To stop this, the inflamed appendix can be removed in an appendectomy.

FRIENDLY BACTERIA

Inside your intestine are trillions of bacteria. These friendly bacteria play an important role in digesting some foods, such as vitamin K, which your body's enzymes cannot digest.

FAECES

About 150 g (5 oz) of faeces is expelled from the body each day. It contains water, bacteria, fats, nitrogen, bile pigments, undigested food and waste products from the blood and intestine walls.

MAKING FAECES

Digestion has largely finished by the time chyme reaches the large intestine and there is only water and some vitamins and minerals left to absorb. Movements along the large intestine push the remaining material into the descending colon and the rectum, where it collects to form faeces. When the rectum has been stretched enough, you'll feel the urge to go to the toilet to get rid of the faeces.

CIRCULATORY SYSTEM

Your body needs a transport system to carry nutrients and oxygen to every cell and then collect and carry waste products away so that they can be expelled from the body before they cause harm. The circulatory system performs this role, while also healing wounds and fighting infection.

The jugular veins carry blood down from the head and brain.

The aorta is the largest blood vessel in your body.

The renal arteries and veins carry blood to and from the kidneys.

The inferior vena cava is the biggest vein in your body and carries blood up from your lower body to your heart.

The femoral artery runs close to your thigh bone.

The saphenous vein is the longest vein in the body and runs from the foot up to the top of your thigh.

BLOOD TRANSFUSION
Blood can be donated by one person and then given to another in a transfusion. This can be used to replace blood lost in an injury or during surgery. The donated blood is stored in special bags before being put into the patient. However, any donated blood must be from a compatible blood group (see page 59) to the patient.

BLOOD SPEED
Blood flows through the body at an average speed of 4.5–6 kph (3–4 mph). It can travel from the heart, around the body and back to the heart in less than a minute.

The carotid arteries carry blood up to the head and brain.

The heart pumps blood around the circulatory system.

The pulmonary arteries and veins carry blood to and from the lungs.

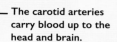

DOUBLE LOOP

The circulatory system is made up of two parts, both of which start at the heart. The pulmonary circulation carries blood from the heart to the lungs where it collects oxygen and releases carbon dioxide, before travelling back to the heart. The oxygenated blood then enters the systemic circulation, which carries blood from the heart to the body's cells where it releases oxygen (and other nutrients) and collects waste carbon dioxide, before travelling back to the heart to begin the process again.

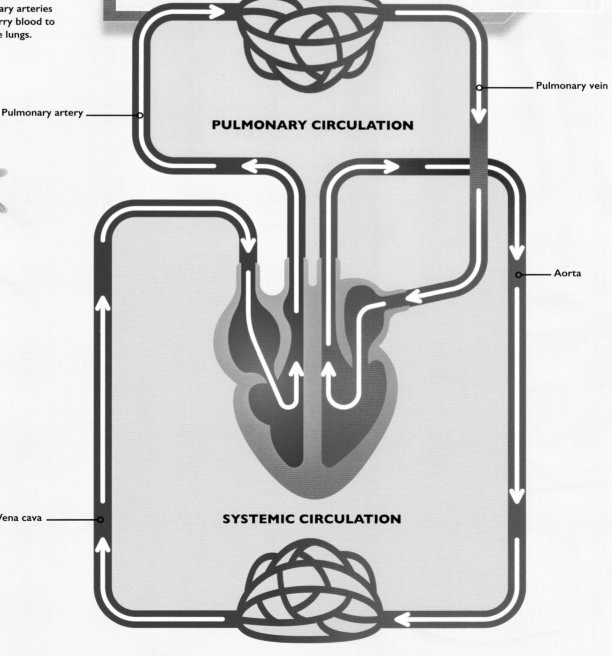

LUNG CAPILLARIES

Pulmonary vein

Pulmonary artery

PULMONARY CIRCULATION

Aorta

Vena cava

SYSTEMIC CIRCULATION

BODY AND ORGAN CAPILLARIES

WHAT'S IN BLOOD?

While your blood may look like a red liquid, it is actually made up of lots of different cells that are carried in a liquid called plasma. The colour comes from the red blood cells, but there are also white blood cells and tiny platelets.

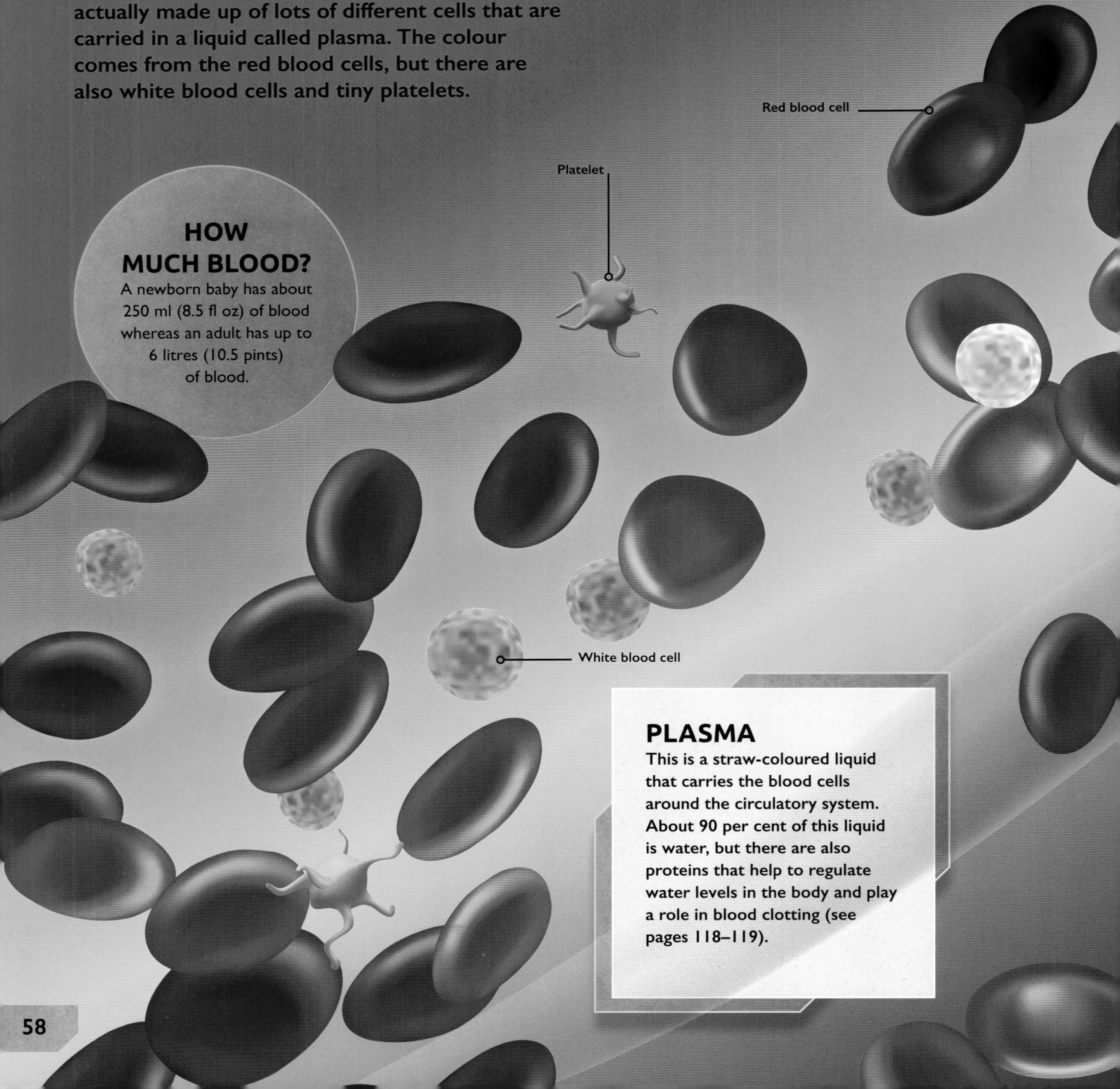

Red blood cell

Platelet

HOW MUCH BLOOD?

A newborn baby has about 250 ml (8.5 fl oz) of blood whereas an adult has up to 6 litres (10.5 pints) of blood.

White blood cell

PLASMA

This is a straw-coloured liquid that carries the blood cells around the circulatory system. About 90 per cent of this liquid is water, but there are also proteins that help to regulate water levels in the body and play a role in blood clotting (see pages 118–119).

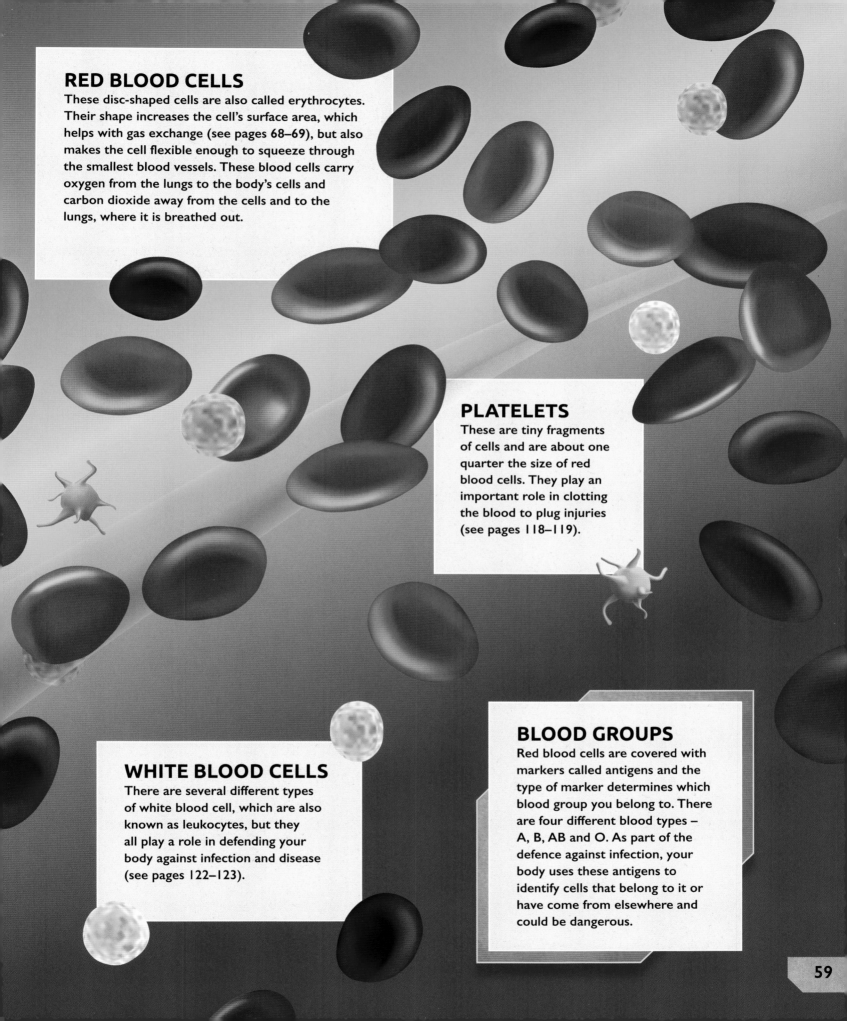

RED BLOOD CELLS

These disc-shaped cells are also called erythrocytes. Their shape increases the cell's surface area, which helps with gas exchange (see pages 68–69), but also makes the cell flexible enough to squeeze through the smallest blood vessels. These blood cells carry oxygen from the lungs to the body's cells and carbon dioxide away from the cells and to the lungs, where it is breathed out.

PLATELETS

These are tiny fragments of cells and are about one quarter the size of red blood cells. They play an important role in clotting the blood to plug injuries (see pages 118–119).

WHITE BLOOD CELLS

There are several different types of white blood cell, which are also known as leukocytes, but they all play a role in defending your body against infection and disease (see pages 122–123).

BLOOD GROUPS

Red blood cells are covered with markers called antigens and the type of marker determines which blood group you belong to. There are four different blood types – A, B, AB and O. As part of the defence against infection, your body uses these antigens to identify cells that belong to it or have come from elsewhere and could be dangerous.

BLOOD VESSELS

Blood flows through a network of tubes called blood vessels. These vessels differ in size and structure depending on where they are and the pressure of the blood they are carrying.

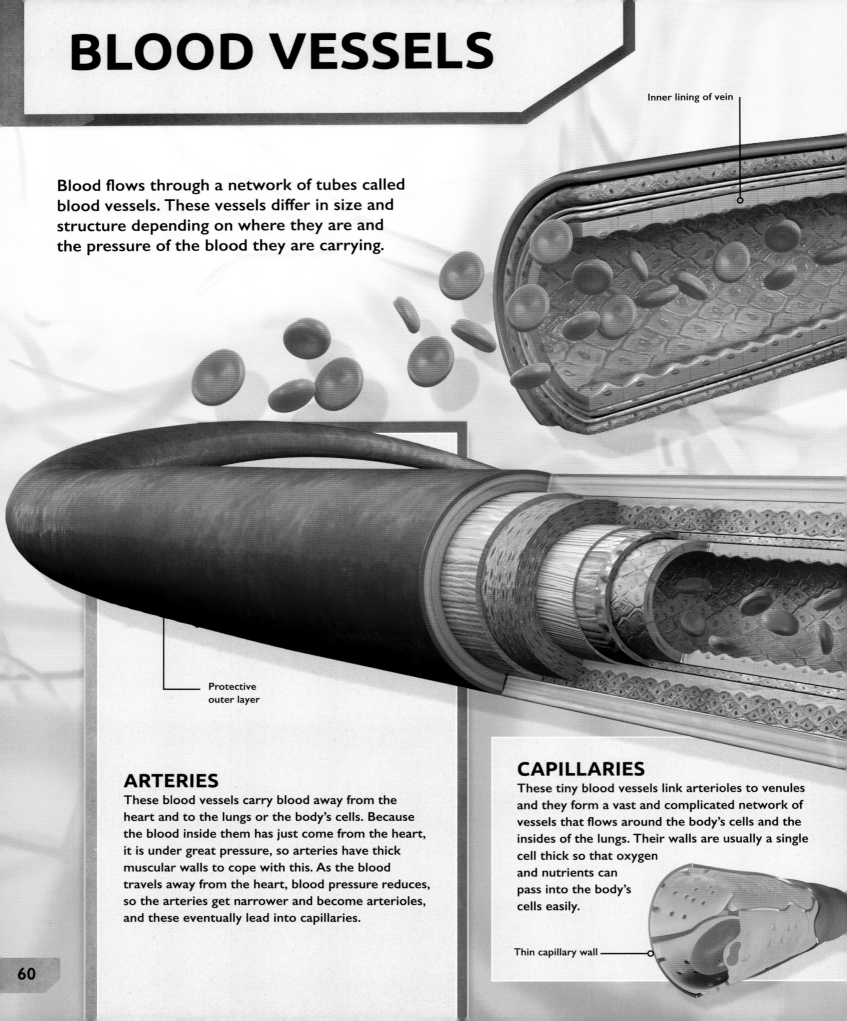

Inner lining of vein

Protective outer layer

ARTERIES

These blood vessels carry blood away from the heart and to the lungs or the body's cells. Because the blood inside them has just come from the heart, it is under great pressure, so arteries have thick muscular walls to cope with this. As the blood travels away from the heart, blood pressure reduces, so the arteries get narrower and become arterioles, and these eventually lead into capillaries.

CAPILLARIES

These tiny blood vessels link arterioles to venules and they form a vast and complicated network of vessels that flows around the body's cells and the insides of the lungs. Their walls are usually a single cell thick so that oxygen and nutrients can pass into the body's cells easily.

Thin capillary wall

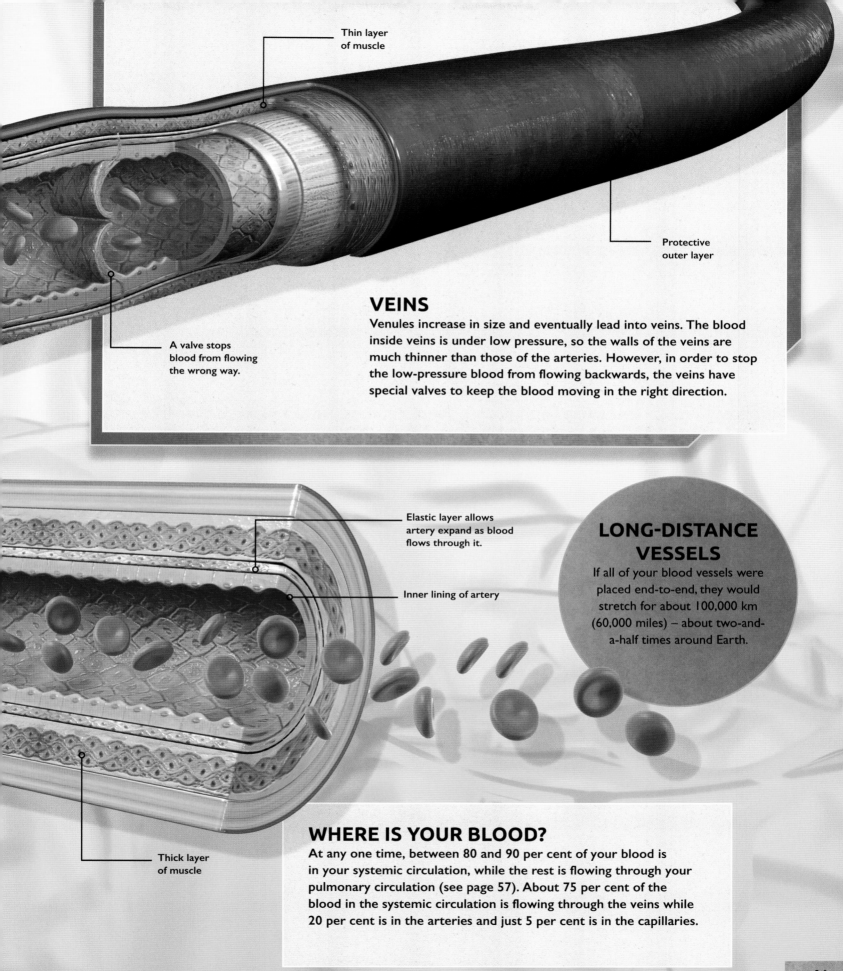

Thin layer of muscle

Protective outer layer

A valve stops blood from flowing the wrong way.

VEINS

Venules increase in size and eventually lead into veins. The blood inside veins is under low pressure, so the walls of the veins are much thinner than those of the arteries. However, in order to stop the low-pressure blood from flowing backwards, the veins have special valves to keep the blood moving in the right direction.

Elastic layer allows artery expand as blood flows through it.

Inner lining of artery

Thick layer of muscle

LONG-DISTANCE VESSELS

If all of your blood vessels were placed end-to-end, they would stretch for about 100,000 km (60,000 miles) – about two-and-a-half times around Earth.

WHERE IS YOUR BLOOD?

At any one time, between 80 and 90 per cent of your blood is in your systemic circulation, while the rest is flowing through your pulmonary circulation (see page 57). About 75 per cent of the blood in the systemic circulation is flowing through the veins while 20 per cent is in the arteries and just 5 per cent is in the capillaries.

THE HEART

At the centre of the circulatory system is the ever-beating heart. Every moment of the day and night, this bag of muscle pumps to push blood to your lungs and around your body. It can even change the rate at which it beats to match the demands of your body, should certain parts need more blood or less.

POWER PUMP

Your heart is divided into two halves. The right half receives blood from the body's cells and pushes it back out towards the lungs. The left half receives blood from the lungs and pushes it out to the body's cells. Each half is divided into two chambers, called the atria and ventricles. The atria sit at the top of each half and below these are the ventricles. Each chamber has valves that stop blood flowing the wrong way.

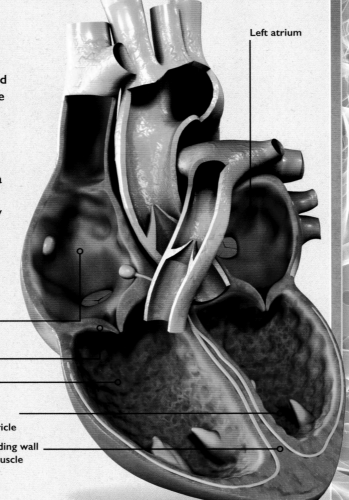

Left atrium

Right atrium

Valve

Right ventricle

Left ventricle

Dividing wall of muscle

FLOWING AROUND THE HEART

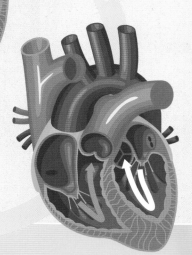

Blood flows into the two atria from the large veins.

The walls of the ventricles contract, increasing the pressure of the blood. This closes the valves from the atria and pushes the blood into the arteries.

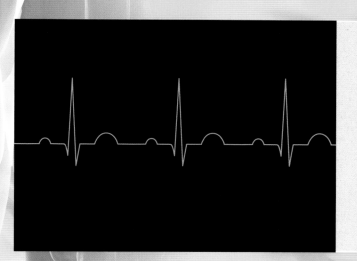

The walls of the atria contract and push the blood down into the two ventricles.

FEELING A PULSE

Each beat of your heart sends waves of pressure through the circulatory system. You can feel these by taking your pulse, gently placing your fingers at spots where blood vessels are close to the skin, such as the wrists and the sides of the neck. In a hospital, medics will use an ECG to see how the heart is performing. This monitors the electrical activity of your heart and displays it as a wave (see left).

THE HEART'S BLOOD FLOW

The cardiac muscle tissue (see pages 30–31) that makes up the walls of the heart never stops beating and never gets tired. In order to do this, it needs its own supply of blood to bring it oxygen and nutrients. However, a diet that is high in certain fats can cause these blood vessels to become blocked. This deprives the heart's muscles of oxygen and nutrients, leading to damage and even a cardiac arrest ('heart attack').

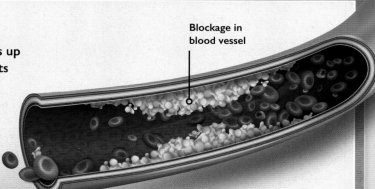

Blockage in blood vessel

CLEANING BLOOD

Located on either side of your lower back are the two kidneys, whose role it is to filter the blood, removing excess water, salts and harmful wastes. These wastes are then removed in urine when you go to the toilet.

The outer part of the kidney is called the cortex.

FILTERING THE BLOOD

Blood travelling into a kidney is carried to the outer layer, or cortex, where it then passes to one of hundreds of thousands of tiny filtering units called nephrons. These take out the waste elements to produce urine. The filtered blood then leaves the kidneys to travel back to the heart.

Urine collects in the hollow renal pelvis.

Renal artery carries blood to the kidney.

Renal vein carries blood away from the kidney.

HOW MUCH URINE?
A normal healthy adult will pass up to 1800 ml (3 pints) of urine every day.

Ureter carries urine to the bladder.

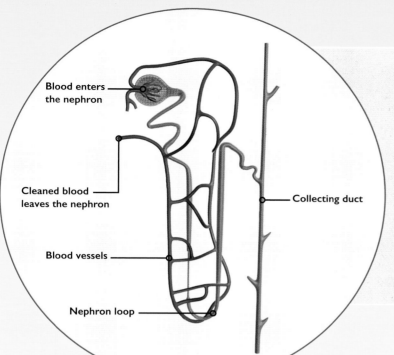

Blood enters
the nephron

Cleaned blood
leaves the nephron

Collecting duct

Blood vessels

Nephron loop

MAKING URINE

As the blood enters a nephron, water and
dissolved substances (but not blood cells) pass
into a thin tube which forms a long thin loop.
As the liquid passes along the tube, much of
the water and any useful substances, such as
glucose, are reabsorbed back into the blood,
leaving only unwanted water and wastes.
These collect into larger tubes, called ureters,
which flow out of the kidney and into the
bladder as urine.

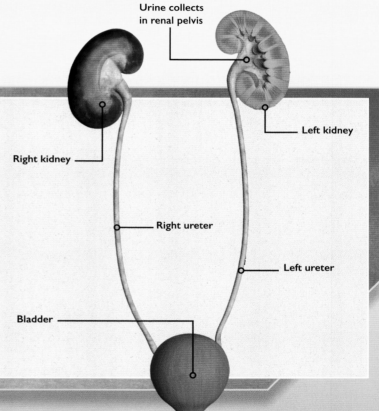

Urine collects
in renal pelvis

Left kidney

Right kidney

Right ureter

Left ureter

Bladder

STORING URINE

Urine collects in a stretchy bag
called the bladder. A bladder
can hold more than 750 ml
(26 fl oz) of urine, but when it
has received about 300–400 ml
(10.5–14 fl oz), stretch sensors
in the bladder produce the
feeling of wanting to go to the
toilet. Urine will then leave the
bladder and pass along another
tube, called the urethra, and out
of the body.

DIALYSIS

In some people, the kidneys do
not function properly, or even
at all. To solve this problem it
is possible to have a kidney
transplant if a suitable donor
is found, or the blood can be
filtered artificially using a
process called dialysis.

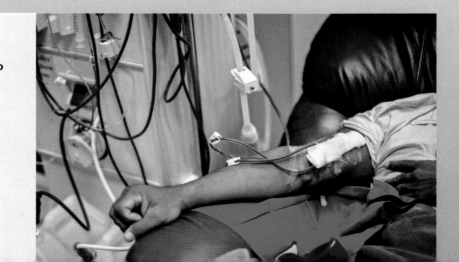

THE LUNGS

Every moment of the day, your lungs fill with air and empty again as you breathe in and out. In doing so you are taking vital oxygen into your body and getting rid of waste carbon dioxide, which could cause harm if too much built up inside you.

Windpipe leads from the mouth and nose down into the chest.

Right bronchus leads into the right lung.

Left bronchus leads into the left lung.

RIGHT LUNG

THE WINDPIPE

Air is breathed in through the nose or the mouth and passes down into the windpipe, or trachea, which is protected by the epiglottis (see pages 48–49). The windpipe is kept open by rings of cartilage that stop it from closing while you breathe.

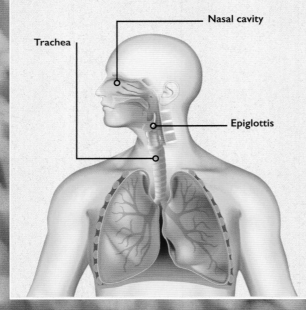

Nasal cavity

Trachea

Epiglottis

INTO THE LUNGS

The windpipe eventually divides into two smaller airways called bronchi with one going into each of the lungs. These divide over and over again, like the branches on a tree, into smaller and smaller tubes, called bronchioles, before eventually ending at microscopic alveoli.

Bronchioles

PROTECTING THE LUNGS

The walls of your airways are covered with slimy mucus to trap dust and foreign objects that you might breathe up. Also on the walls are tiny hair-like structures called cilia (main image). These move in waves to push the mucus and anything trapped in it up to the back of the throat, where it is swallowed and destroyed by the powerful acids in the stomach.

Cross-section through cluster of alveoli

Blood supply around alveoli

External view of a cluster of alveoli and blood vessels

ALVEOLI

Looking like tiny bunches of grapes, the alveoli form the ends of the airways and they are the sites of gas exchange in the lungs. Oxygen from the breathed-in air passes through the walls of the alveoli and into the blood capillaries surrounding them. At the same time, carbon dioxide passes the other way and into the air in the lungs, which is then breathed out.

Oxygen moves into the blood.

Carbon dioxide moves into the air inside the lungs.

BREATHE IN, BREATHE OUT

With each breath, you draw air into your nose or mouth, down into your lungs and then push it out again. However, your lungs cannot move on their own and they rely on a system of muscles and bones to make them larger to pull air in, and then squeeze them to make them smaller and push air out.

ASTHMA

Asthma is a narrowing and clogging of the airways that makes breathing hard. Scientists don't know exactly what causes the condition. It may be inherited or caused by pollution.

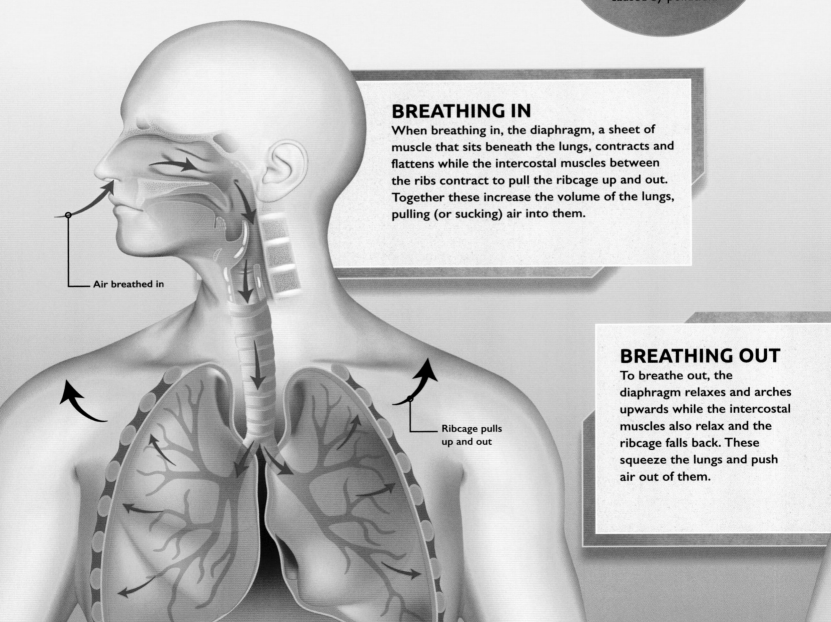

Air breathed in

BREATHING IN

When breathing in, the diaphragm, a sheet of muscle that sits beneath the lungs, contracts and flattens while the intercostal muscles between the ribs contract to pull the ribcage up and out. Together these increase the volume of the lungs, pulling (or sucking) air into them.

Ribcage pulls up and out

BREATHING OUT

To breathe out, the diaphragm relaxes and arches upwards while the intercostal muscles also relax and the ribcage falls back. These squeeze the lungs and push air out of them.

Diaphragm contracts and flattens

VOICEBOX

Located close to the top of the windpipe is a structure called the larynx, inside which are the vocal folds, or vocal cords. As air passes over these, they vibrate to produce the sounds of your voice. The pitch, volume and type of sound made by the vocal folds is controlled by complicated muscle movements.

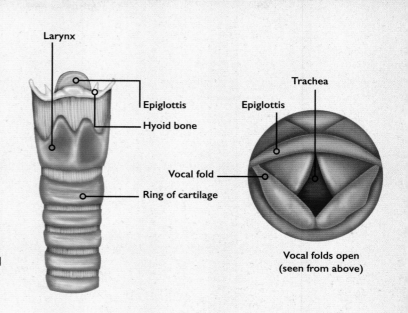

Larynx
Epiglottis
Hyoid bone
Ring of cartilage

Trachea
Epiglottis
Vocal fold

Vocal folds open
(seen from above)

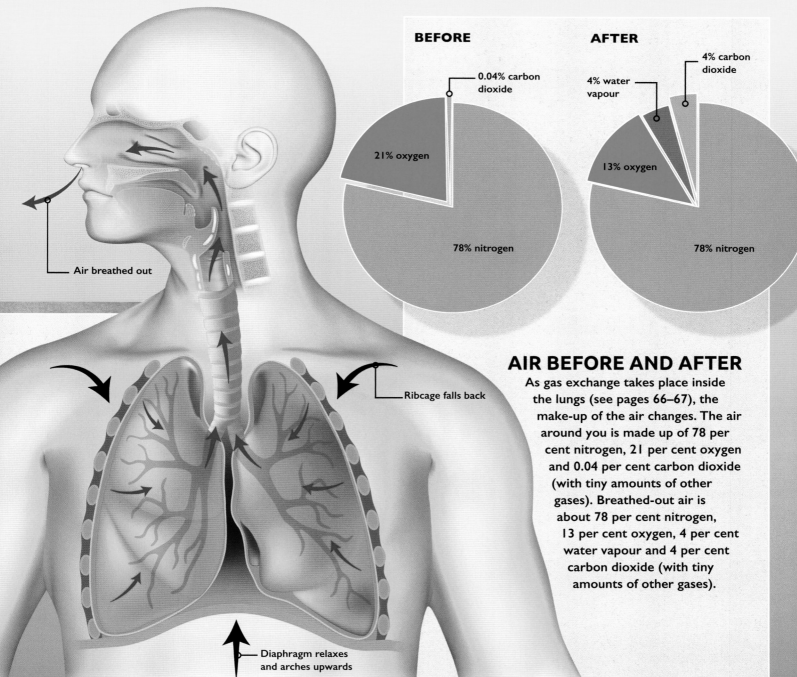

Air breathed out

Ribcage falls back

Diaphragm relaxes and arches upwards

BEFORE

0.04% carbon dioxide

21% oxygen

78% nitrogen

AFTER

4% water vapour

4% carbon dioxide

13% oxygen

78% nitrogen

AIR BEFORE AND AFTER

As gas exchange takes place inside the lungs (see pages 66–67), the make-up of the air changes. The air around you is made up of 78 per cent nitrogen, 21 per cent oxygen and 0.04 per cent carbon dioxide (with tiny amounts of other gases). Breathed-out air is about 78 per cent nitrogen, 13 per cent oxygen, 4 per cent water vapour and 4 per cent carbon dioxide (with tiny amounts of other gases).

69

RESPIRATION

Once the glucose from your digested food has been absorbed, you have breathed oxygen into your lungs and it has moved into your blood, vital chemicals are transported to every cell in your body. Once in the cells, they are used in a process called respiration to release the energy stored inside them.

WHAT IS RESPIRATION?

Respiration is the chemical reaction that combines glucose with oxygen to release the energy stored inside the simple sugar. It takes place inside the mitochondria – tiny organelles that are inside cells.

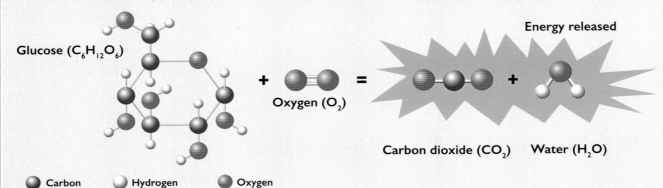

Glucose ($C_6H_{12}O_6$)

+ Oxygen (O_2) =

Energy released

Carbon dioxide (CO_2)   Water (H_2O)

● Carbon   ○ Hydrogen   ● Oxygen

The waste carbon dioxide and water pass out of the cells and back into the blood where they are carried to the lungs to be breathed out.

This type of respiration is called aerobic respiration because it uses oxygen.

ANAEROBIC RESPIRATION

If you exercise very vigorously, your body might not be able to get enough oxygen to its cells. In this case, the cells will use respiration without oxygen, called anaerobic respiration. This produces a chemical called lactic acid, which makes the muscles feel tired and can lead to cramp.

BREATHING RATES

Just as the heart varies its rate to match the demands of your body, so too does the rate at which you breathe. Normally you will breathe about 12 to 15 times a minute, but if you are exercising then you will breathe faster as your body tries to take in more oxygen.

CONTROL AND SENSES
NERVES AND HORMONES

Every moment of the day, our bodies are bombarded with a massive amount of information, whether it's images of the world around us, smells that come wafting over the air, sounds from nearby traffic or tastes from the food we eat. Your body has to process all of this information and then decide how best to respond. Sometimes, you make a conscious decision about the best response, but most of the time, your body is carrying out thousands of actions and changes without you realising.

The nervous system is your body's information network. It carries signals from sensors all around your body, telling you about what you're seeing, hearing, smelling, tasting and touching. It even tells you which way up you are.

Hormones are special chemicals that are made by various organs around the body, which together form the endocrine system. Released into the bloodstream, these chemicals control conditions in the body, such as levels of sugar in the blood, or actions, including the desire to stand and fight or to run away.

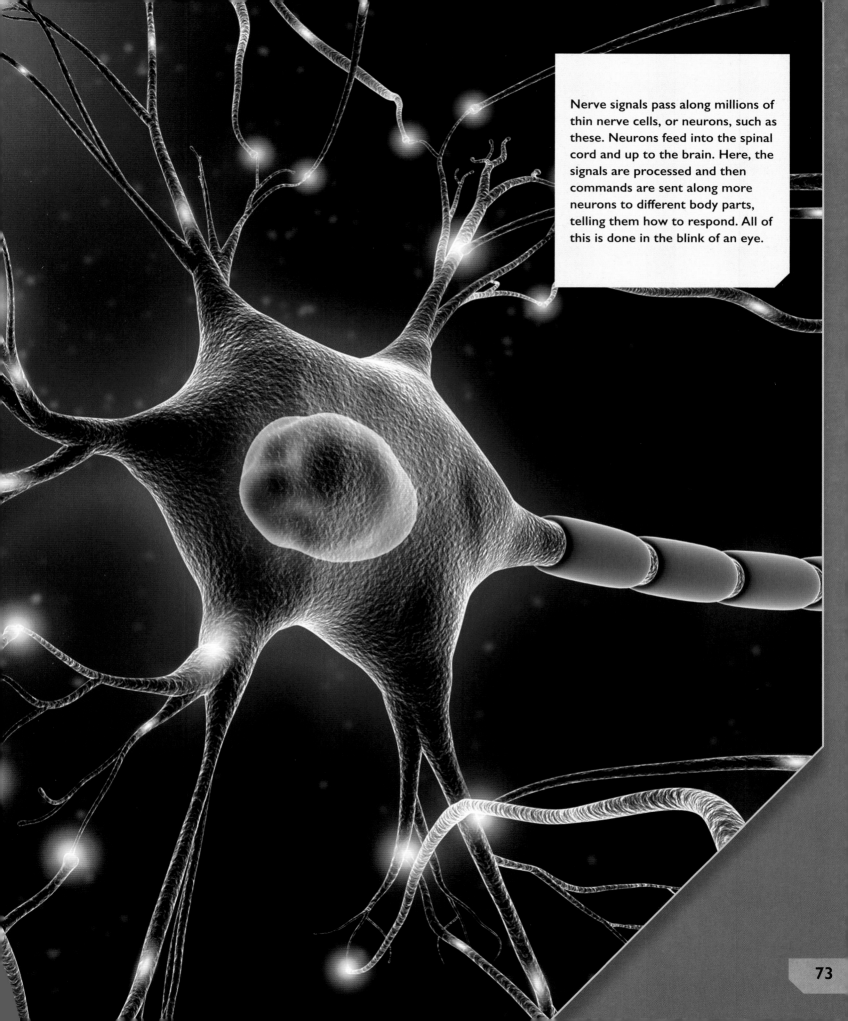

Nerve signals pass along millions of thin nerve cells, or neurons, such as these. Neurons feed into the spinal cord and up to the brain. Here, the signals are processed and then commands are sent along more neurons to different body parts, telling them how to respond. All of this is done in the blink of an eye.

THE NERVOUS SYSTEM

Centred around the brain and the spinal cord, the cells of the nervous system reach every part of your body. They transmit tiny bio-electrical signals that carry information to the brain about the outside world and what's happening inside your body, as well as commands from the brain to various body parts, telling them how to react.

Brain

Spinal cord

CONTROL NETWORK

The cells of the nervous system form a thin network of fibres running through your body, from the tips of your toes to the top of your head. These carry signals that can travel at hundreds of kilometres an hour, moving from your brain to the tips of your toes in about one hundredth of a second.

The brain is the body's control centre and it is made up of billions of tightly packed nerve cells. It sits on top of the spinal cord. The spinal cord runs from the base of the brain and down the back to the pelvis. It is protected by the different vertebrae in the spine.

NERVE BUNDLES

Nerves are the cables of the nervous system, and they are formed by bundles of long nerve axons (see pages 76–77) that are surrounded and protected by a tough covering.

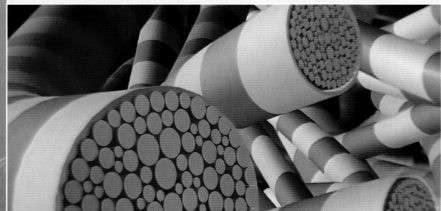

NERVOUS SYSTEM PARTS

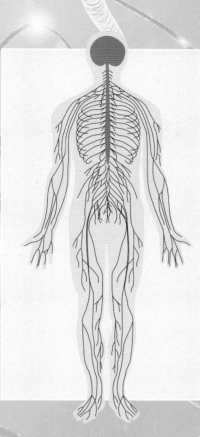

The nervous system is split into two parts. The central nervous system (shown in red) is made up of the brain and the spinal cord. The peripheral nervous system (shown in blue) is made up of the network of nerve cells that run throughout the body. Nerve cells that carry signals to the brain are called sensory nerves, while those that carry signals away from the brain are called motor nerves.

LONG NERVES

The longest nerve in the body is the sciatic nerve, which runs from the bottom of the spinal cord to the foot.

SPEEDY SIGNALS

Nerve signals need to be quick to respond to sudden changes in the world around you and events inside your body. These messages zip along at speeds of about 350 kph (220 mph). This is fast, but it isn't instantaneous. For example, if a sprinter leaves the blocks less than 0.1 seconds after the starting gun, then it is judged a false start. This is because it would take that amount of time for the nerve signals triggered by the sound of the starting pistol to travel from the ears, to the brain and then on to the leg muscles – any earlier than that and the runner must have started to race too early!

NERVE CELLS AND SIGNALS

Nerve cells, or neurons, form a complex network throughout the body with billions of thread-like strands carrying signals from one nerve cell to another.

SUPPORT CELLS
The nervous system contains hundreds of billions of specialist supporting cells, whose job it is to protect and nurture the neurons.

Dendrite endings receive signals from other nerve cells, or carry signals from sensory receptors.

NERVE CELL SHAPE

Nerve cells vary greatly in terms of shape and size depending on where they are in the body, but they all have three basic parts. The cell body is the main part of the cell and it contains the nucleus, which holds the cell's genetic information, and other organelles. Sticking out from the cell body are two types of strand – axons and dendrites. Dendrites spread out like the branches on a tree and they carry nerve signals towards the cell body. A nerve cell usually only has one axon that carries a signal away from the cell body. Axons vary in size from just a few millimetres to about a metre long.

The gap between two sections of myelin sheath is called a node of Ranvier

The axon branches to form links with other nerve cells.

Myelin sheath wraps around the axon.

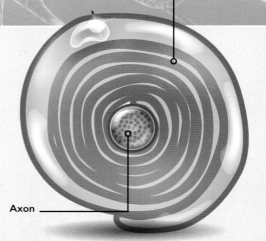

INSULATION

Some axons are wrapped in a special insulation called a myelin sheath. Made from special cells called Schwann cells, this sheath wraps around the axon and protects it. In doing so, it allows the axon to send nerve signals faster than an unprotected neuron.

Axon branches end with a synapse.

Axon

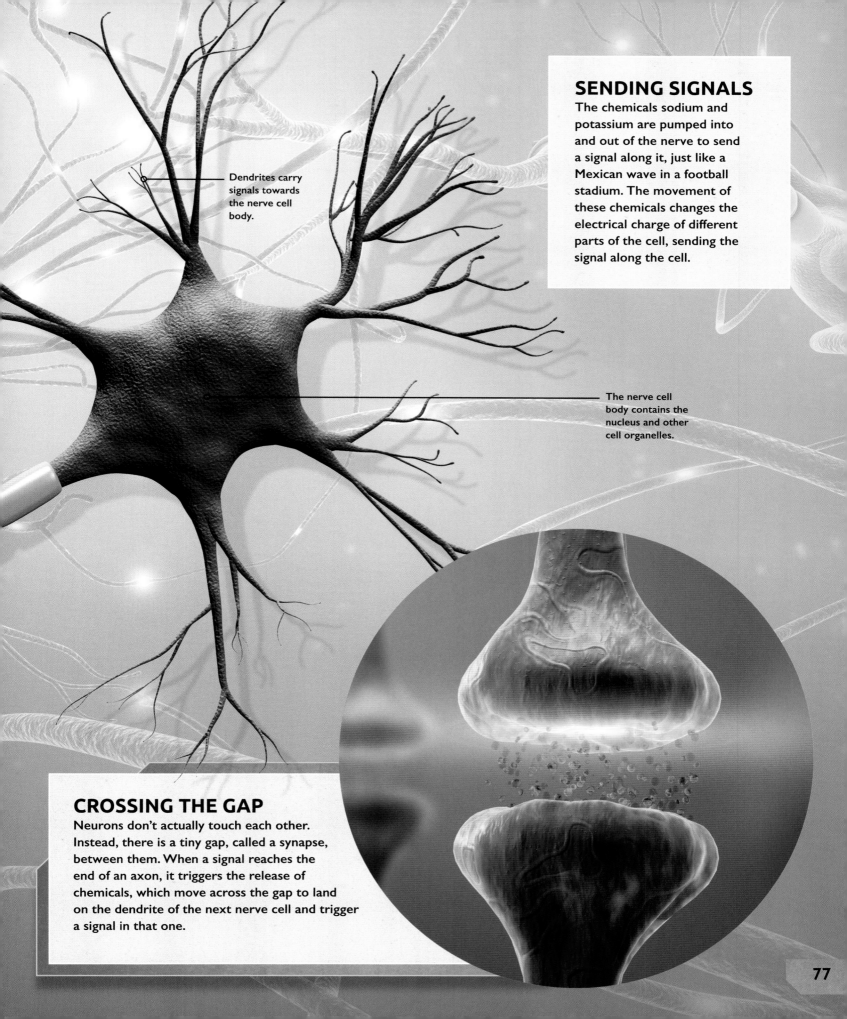

Dendrites carry signals towards the nerve cell body.

SENDING SIGNALS
The chemicals sodium and potassium are pumped into and out of the nerve to send a signal along it, just like a Mexican wave in a football stadium. The movement of these chemicals changes the electrical charge of different parts of the cell, sending the signal along the cell.

The nerve cell body contains the nucleus and other cell organelles.

CROSSING THE GAP
Neurons don't actually touch each other. Instead, there is a tiny gap, called a synapse, between them. When a signal reaches the end of an axon, it triggers the release of chemicals, which move across the gap to land on the dendrite of the next nerve cell and trigger a signal in that one.

THE BRAIN

Protected by the bony plates of the skull, your brain is the control centre for your body, receiving information, processing it and then telling your body how to react. It is also responsible for how you think, remember and imagine things, as well as controlling your emotions.

CONNECTIONS
The brain contains about 100 billion neurons and each neuron has up to 10,000 synapses, meaning that there may be 1 quadrillion (1,000,000,000,000,000) synapses in the brain.

BRAIN STEM AND CEREBELLUM

Located at the base of the brain are the brain stem and the cerebellum. The cerebellum fine tunes your body movements and your balance, while the brain stem links the brain to the spinal cord and controls many of your body's basic functions, such as your heart rate.

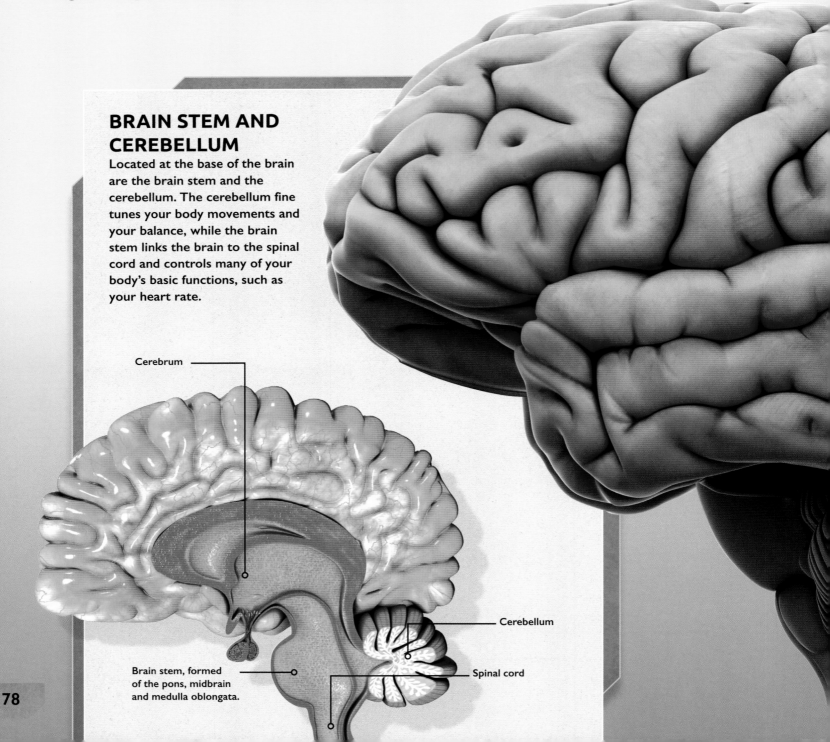

Cerebrum

Cerebellum

Spinal cord

Brain stem, formed of the pons, midbrain and medulla oblongata.

ENERGY HUNGRY

All the thinking and processing done by the brain means that it needs a lot of energy – all of the time! It may only make up about 2 per cent of your body weight, but it uses about 20 per cent of your body's energy. To deliver all of the nutrients and oxygen that your brain needs, it has a rich blood supply, with a network of blood vessels reaching every part.

CEREBRUM

The outer section of the brain, the cerebrum, is also the largest part. Its surface is covered with wrinkles and folds that give it a greater surface area. It is divided into two halves – left and right – and each half is divided into different areas, or lobes. The cerebrum processes information from different sense organs around the body and is also responsible for your actions, speech and feelings.

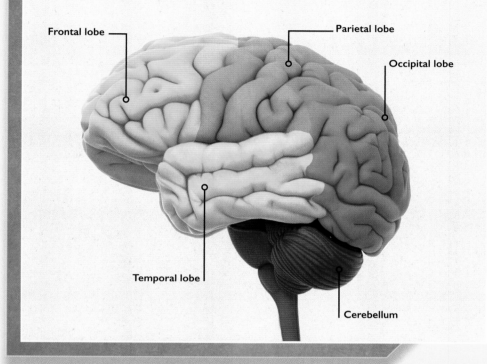

Frontal lobe

Parietal lobe

Occipital lobe

Temporal lobe

Cerebellum

THE CORTEX

Covering the surface of the cerebrum is a thin layer called the cortex. Certain parts of the cortex are responsible for different actions, such as receiving information from different body parts and sense organs. The motor cortex is a thin strip that runs across the cortex and areas of it control different body parts. Some parts of the body that require more control are linked with larger areas of the motor cortex.

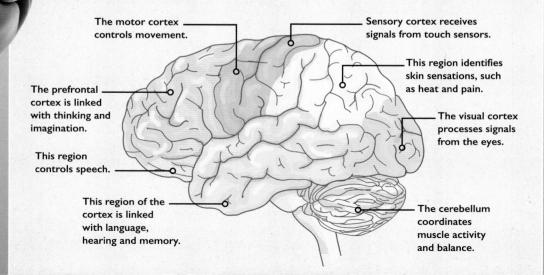

The motor cortex controls movement.

Sensory cortex receives signals from touch sensors.

The prefrontal cortex is linked with thinking and imagination.

This region identifies skin sensations, such as heat and pain.

This region controls speech.

The visual cortex processes signals from the eyes.

This region of the cortex is linked with language, hearing and memory.

The cerebellum coordinates muscle activity and balance.

SPINAL CORD

Running from the base of the brain down to the bottom of your back is the spinal cord. Formed from a mass of nerves and cells, this structure is the main communication route between your brain and the rest of your body.

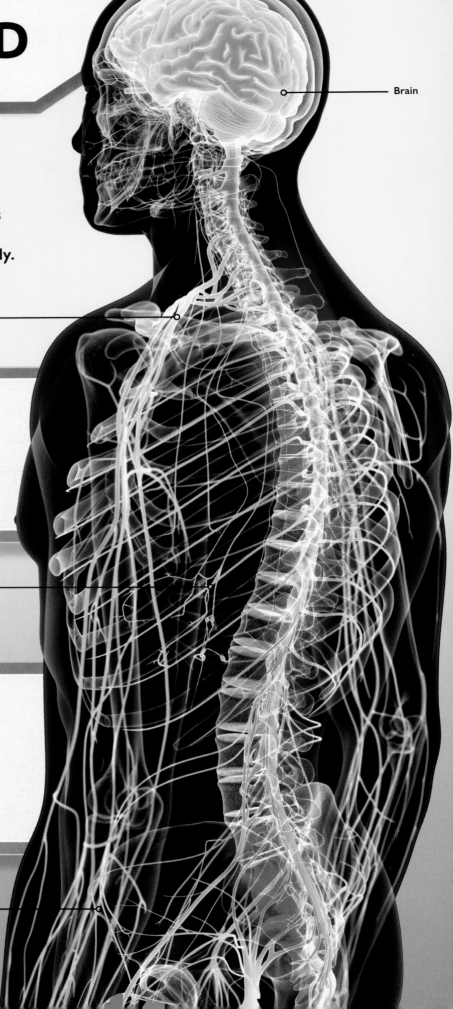

Brain

Nerve branches from the base of the neck run down either arm.

SIGNAL SUPERHIGHWAY

An adult spinal cord is about 45 cm (18 inches) long and about the width of a finger. It contains billions of nerve cells down the middle of your back, before tapering off at the bottom of your spine.

Nerve branches from the middle of the spinal cord run around the chest and torso.

BRANCHES

Emerging from the spinal cord as it runs down the back are pairs of spinal nerves, sprouting to each side of the spinal cord. These branch out and run to every part of the body, carrying signals to and from the brain.

Nerve branches from the bottom of the spinal cord run down the legs.

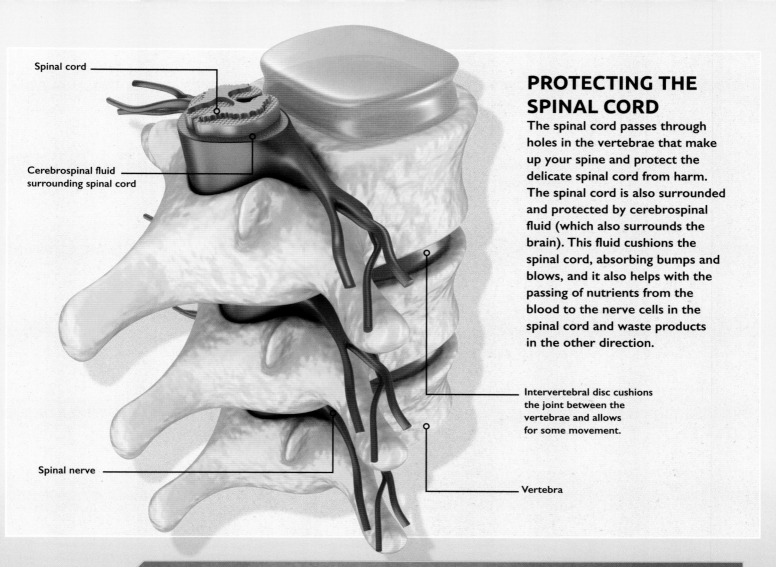

Spinal cord

Cerebrospinal fluid
surrounding spinal cord

Spinal nerve

PROTECTING THE SPINAL CORD

The spinal cord passes through holes in the vertebrae that make up your spine and protect the delicate spinal cord from harm. The spinal cord is also surrounded and protected by cerebrospinal fluid (which also surrounds the brain). This fluid cushions the spinal cord, absorbing bumps and blows, and it also helps with the passing of nutrients from the blood to the nerve cells in the spinal cord and waste products in the other direction.

Intervertebral disc cushions the joint between the vertebrae and allows for some movement.

Vertebra

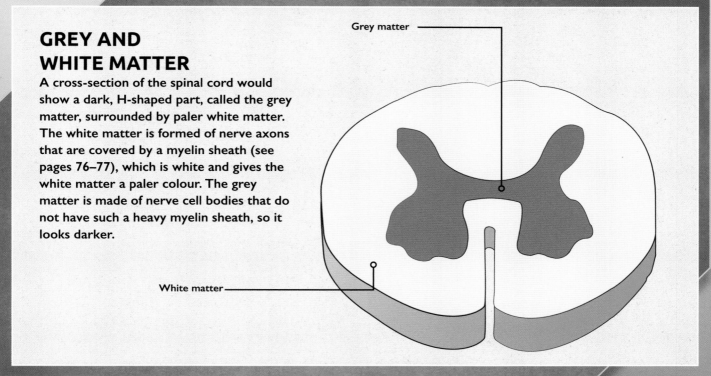

GREY AND WHITE MATTER

A cross-section of the spinal cord would show a dark, H-shaped part, called the grey matter, surrounded by paler white matter. The white matter is formed of nerve axons that are covered by a myelin sheath (see pages 76–77), which is white and gives the white matter a paler colour. The grey matter is made of nerve cell bodies that do not have such a heavy myelin sheath, so it looks darker.

Grey matter

White matter

REFLEX ACTIONS

Not every signal that passes through the spinal cord travels straight to the brain. Some automatic actions occur without your brain having to decide about them. These reflex actions are coordinated by the spinal cord and they will push your body into action without you knowing – you only learn about them later.

REFLEX ARC

Most reflex actions help to quickly protect the body from damage. A signal from a sensor in the body, such as a pain sensor in a finger, travels up a sensory nerve to the spinal cord. The signal passes through intermediate nerves in the spinal cord to a motor nerve, which sends a signal to your arm muscles to pull your finger away from the source of pain. This pathway is called a reflex arc. Your spinal cord will also send a signal to your brain so that you are aware that something painful has happened to your finger.

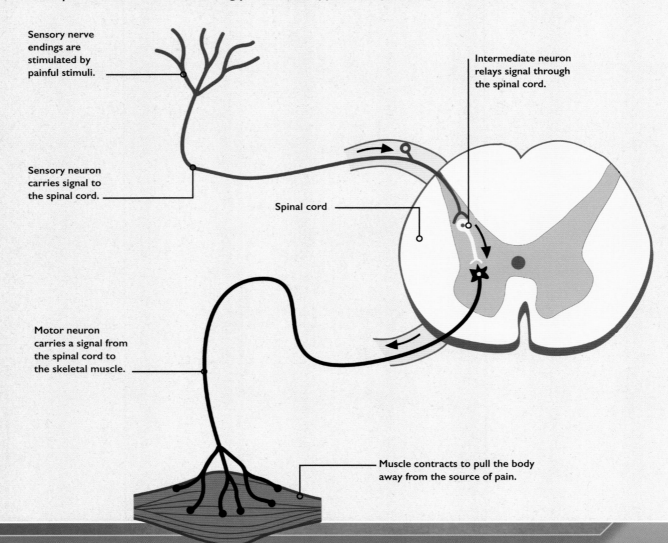

Sensory nerve endings are stimulated by painful stimuli.

Intermediate neuron relays signal through the spinal cord.

Sensory neuron carries signal to the spinal cord.

Spinal cord

Motor neuron carries a signal from the spinal cord to the skeletal muscle.

Muscle contracts to pull the body away from the source of pain.

EXAMPLES OF REFLEXES

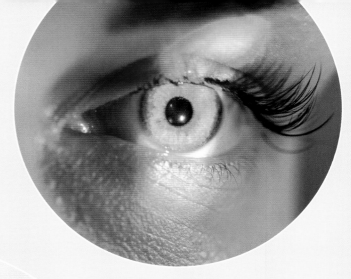

GAG REFLEX

The gag reflex is triggered when something touches the back of your throat. The muscles at the back of the throat constrict to stop the object travelling further and blocking the airway. Sword swallowers need to overcome this reflex to perform their art.

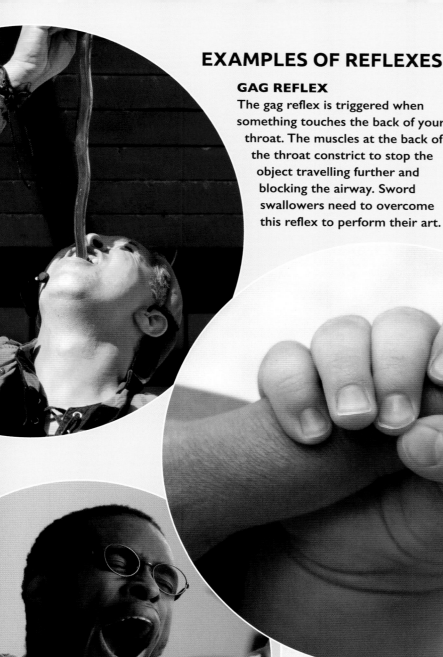

PUPIL REFLEX

The size of the pupil in the middle of your eye automatically adjusts to light levels. It gets bigger when the light is dim and shrinks when light levels increase.

BABY REFLEXES

Babies are born with a number of different reflexes. These include the sucking reflex, which occurs when something touches the roof of the mouth and they begin to suck, so they can feed. Other reflexes stop babies from breathing when underwater to prevent water getting into their lungs and gripping their fist when the palm of the hand is stroked (see above).

STRETCH REFLEX

Some reflexes act to keep your body upright, contracting muscles without you knowing about it. You can see this if someone taps your knee just below the kneecap, or patella. This causes the muscles in the front of the upper leg (called the quadriceps) to contract and pull the foot up.

YAWN

Yawning occurs when you take a deep inhalation and exhalation of breath. This happens more frequently when you are tired.

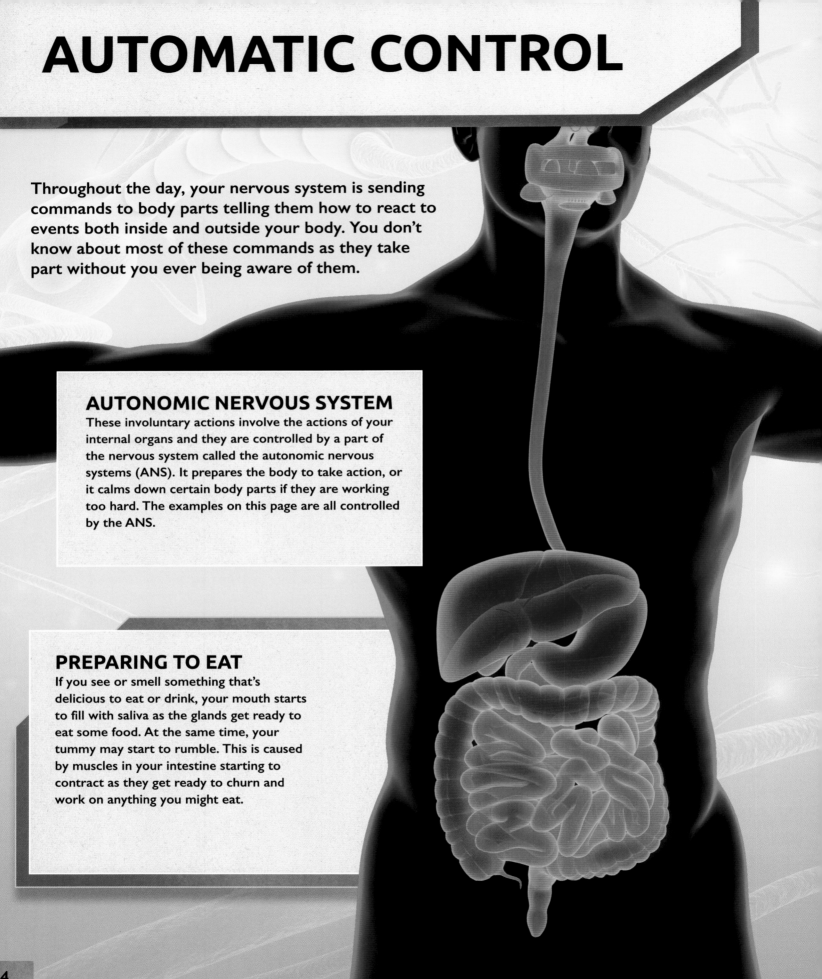

AUTOMATIC CONTROL

Throughout the day, your nervous system is sending commands to body parts telling them how to react to events both inside and outside your body. You don't know about most of these commands as they take part without you ever being aware of them.

AUTONOMIC NERVOUS SYSTEM

These involuntary actions involve the actions of your internal organs and they are controlled by a part of the nervous system called the autonomic nervous systems (ANS). It prepares the body to take action, or it calms down certain body parts if they are working too hard. The examples on this page are all controlled by the ANS.

PREPARING TO EAT

If you see or smell something that's delicious to eat or drink, your mouth starts to fill with saliva as the glands get ready to eat some food. At the same time, your tummy may start to rumble. This is caused by muscles in your intestine starting to contract as they get ready to churn and work on anything you might eat.

FEELING COLD AND HOT

If you feel cold, the ANS will trigger certain actions to try and warm you up. Your body hairs will stand on end to try and trap air and reduce heat loss – this causes goosebumps. Your muscles will start to quickly relax and contract, causing you to shiver which produces heat to warm you up. If you start to feel too warm, then the ANS triggers your sweat glands to produce more sweat, which transfers heat from the body as it evaporates.

REGULATING THE HEART AND BREATHING

Depending on how active you are, the ANS also changes the speed at which your heart and lungs work. If you're exercising, then your muscles need more oxygen and nutrients, so you start to breathe faster and more deeply and your heart rate increases to push more blood around your body.

NEED TO PEE?

The exit to your bladder is closed by two rings of muscle. The first is controlled by your ANS, while the second is controlled consciously by you (and so is a voluntary action). Learning to control this can take a couple of years to learn, which is why young babies wear nappies.

85

SLEEP WELL

With all the effort your body goes through during the day, it needs to rest and recharge regularly and it does this when it sleeps. But even when you are asleep, your brain is still active as it passes through various levels in a sleep cycle.

SLEEP CYCLE

During a long sleep, you will pass through different stages, or levels of sleep, in repeated cycles that are about 80–120 minutes long. These stages are:

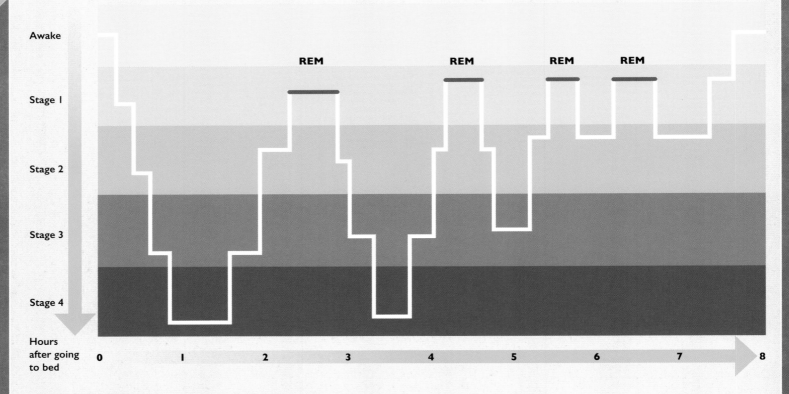

Awake   – when you are aware of your surroundings.

Stage 1 – the lightest form of sleep, when you feel drowsy. This usually lasts less than 5 minutes.

Stage 2 – your heart and breathing rates decrease, your body temperature falls and your eyes remain still.

Stage 3 – a stage between light and deep sleep, when breathing, heart rate, temperature and blood pressure decrease.

Stage 4 – the deepest stage of the sleep cycle when heart and breathing rates may be 20–30 per cent below their waking levels. This usually lasts for about 30 minutes.

REM sleep – known as rapid eye movement sleep, your eyes twitch about beneath the eyelids and this stage is when dreams occur.

HOW MUCH SLEEP?

The amount of sleep you need decreases as you get older. A newborn baby may sleep for 16 hours a day, while an adult may only sleep for seven hours or even less.

A lack of sleep can lead to a decrease in alertness and and increase in sleepiness during the day, impaired memory, and increased stress levels and blood pressure. Prolonged sleep deprivation can lead to long-term problems, including diabetes, obesity, heart attack, heart failure or stroke.

DREAMS

No-one knows for certain why people dream, but the average person may have three or four dreams a night, with each dream lasting for 10 minutes or more. Dreams can often involve impossible actions or bizarre settings, such as flying.

MEMORY

Can you remember what you did yesterday? How about last year or even the year before? While your brain is busy every minute you're awake collecting information, it only remembers some of it, keeping it in special memory centres in the brain, while discarding the other parts it doesn't want.

LONG-TERM MEMORIES

These are memories that the brain stores for a long time, possibly even your whole life. They are stored in different parts of the brain. For example, exciting events are stored in the hippocampus and parts of the cortex, while skills, such as playing a musical instrument or riding a bicycle, are stored in the cerebellum, and facts are stored in the temporal lobes on the sides of the brain.

MEMORY PARTS OF THE BRAIN

No single part of the brain is involved in making and storing memories, but several work together, playing different roles. These include:

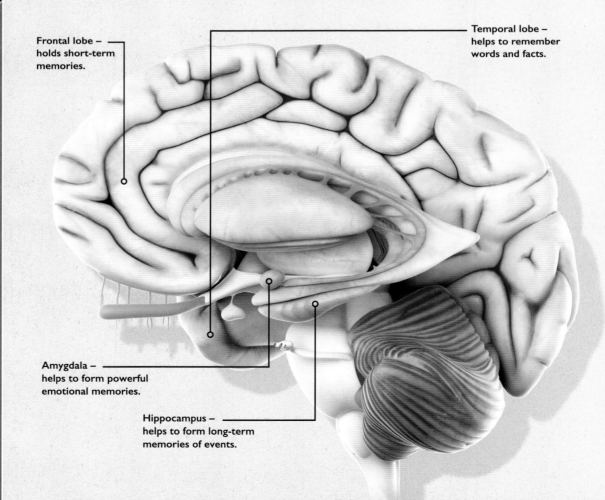

Frontal lobe – holds short-term memories.

Temporal lobe – helps to remember words and facts.

Amygdala – helps to form powerful emotional memories.

Hippocampus – helps to form long-term memories of events.

SPARKING SYNAPSES

Every time you experience something, signals fire through your brain cells in specific patterns. When you remember that same experience, you trigger signals in exactly the same pattern and the more often you fire this pattern, the easier it is to remember the experience.

SHORT-TERM MEMORIES

These are memories that are formed by recent events but aren't important enough to store forever. They will only last a few seconds and, if the memory isn't used again, then the brain deletes it. Short-term memories include what you just had for lunch or a detail from a book that you've just been reading.

THE MIND AND PERSONALITY

Writing with your left hand indicates that the right side of your brain may be dominant.

While your brain controls your body, it also creates your personality, overseeing your emotions, thoughts, feelings and memories, and making you the character you are.

LOGICAL-MATHEMATICAL INTELLIGENCE

– someone who can solve maths problems easily, but who is also good at solving puzzles, has a logical brain and can see how gadgets and computers work.

LINGUISTIC INTELLIGENCE

– someone who is very good with language and writing and can absorb a lot of information from written sources, such as books.

INTELLIGENCE

Being intelligent doesn't just mean that you can remember lots of facts and figures. Instead, there are many different forms of intelligence.

BODY INTELLIGENCE

– someone who is very good at physical abilities, including sports and other practical or hands-on activities.

SPATIAL INTELLIGENCE

– someone who is good at visualising objects or situations.

INTERPERSONAL INTELLIGENCE

– someone who is good at relating to and understanding other people.

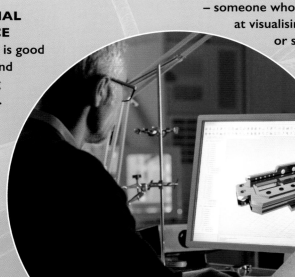

LEFT OR RIGHT?

The outer part of your brain is divided into two halves; left and right. The left half of the brain controls the right side of your body and the right half of your brain controls your body's left side. One side of your brain is usually dominant, which means that you will usually favour using one hand and foot over the other.

The two sides of the brain are usually responsible for different jobs. For example, the right side of your brain will help you use words, controls routine tasks and is better at working with numbers and thinking logically. The left side of the brain will control how you speak, how you view and interpret 3-D objects, and help you to recognise everyday objects.

OUTGOING OR RESERVED?

People can have very different personalities, depending on their character. Conscientious people are reliable and hard-working and will always try to do their best. Extroverts are confident and talk a lot and love being around other people (while introverts are the opposite). Some neurotic people are highly strung and get upset easily, while others are calm and relaxed. Some people are agreeable and get on well with others, while others can be argumentative.

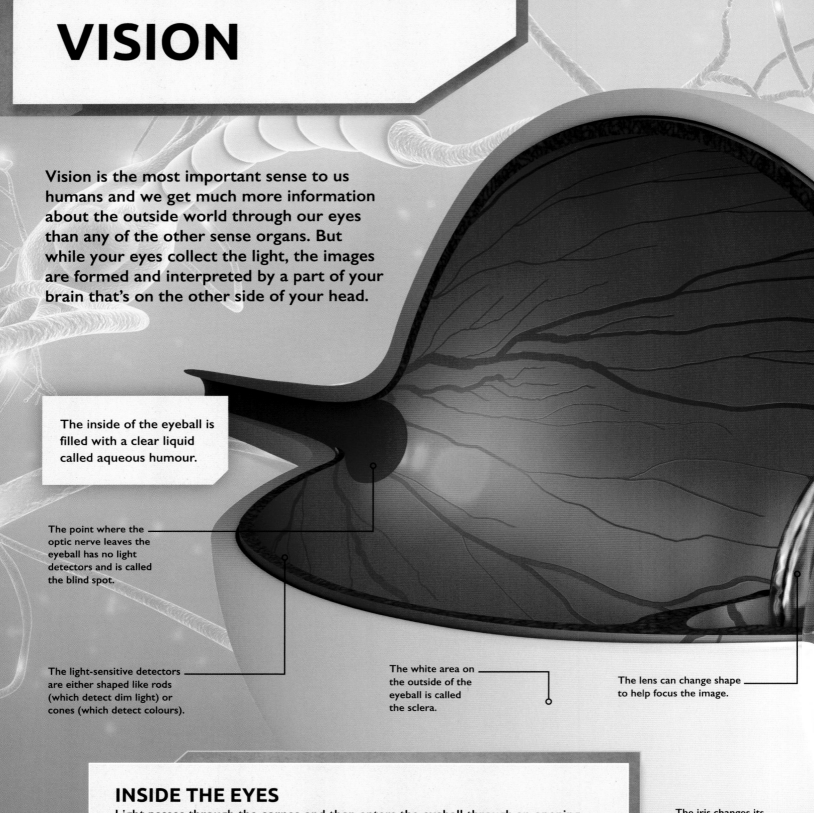

VISION

Vision is the most important sense to us humans and we get much more information about the outside world through our eyes than any of the other sense organs. But while your eyes collect the light, the images are formed and interpreted by a part of your brain that's on the other side of your head.

The inside of the eyeball is filled with a clear liquid called aqueous humour.

The point where the optic nerve leaves the eyeball has no light detectors and is called the blind spot.

The light-sensitive detectors are either shaped like rods (which detect dim light) or cones (which detect colours).

The white area on the outside of the eyeball is called the sclera.

The lens can change shape to help focus the image.

INSIDE THE EYES

Light passes through the cornea and then enters the eyeball through an opening called the pupil. This can get bigger or smaller to let in more or less light. After passing through the lens, light hits the back of the eyeball, called the retina, where there are millions of light-sensitive detectors. When the light hits these detectors, it triggers nerve signals which pass down the optic nerve to the brain.

The iris changes its size to make the pupil larger or smaller.

MESSAGES TO THE BRAIN

Signals from the retina pass along the optic nerves, into the brain and to a region at the back called the visual cortex. Here, the information is interpreted and an image formed.

Left visual field

Right visual field

Binocular vision

Pituitary gland

Optic nerves

Optic chiasm

Left visual cortex

Right visual cortex

The cornea is the clear covering at the front of the eye, which does most of the focussing.

SEEING IN 3-D

Because the eyeballs are positioned slightly apart, they produce a slightly different image to each other. The brain puts these two images together to create a three-dimensional picture of the world.

Binocular vision

Left eye view

Right eye view

KEEPING EYES HEALTHY

Eating dark, leafy green vegetables, such as spinach and kale, as well as oily fish, such as salmon and mackerel, helps to keep your eyes healthy. It's also important to have your vision checked regularly to check for any problems before they can develop.

TRICKING THE EYE

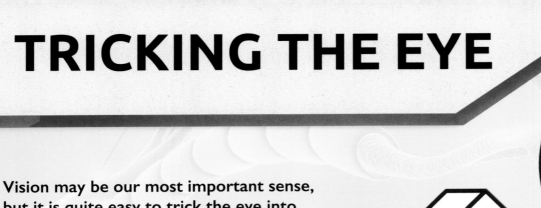

Vision may be our most important sense, but it is quite easy to trick the eye into seeing something that isn't there or that can't exist.

AMBIGUOUS IMAGES

Sometime a single image looks like it holds two different pictures – at the same time! For example, does this image show two faces looking at each other or does it show a black vase?

IMPOSSIBLE IMAGES

If you look closely at these three-dimensional shapes, you'll see that none of them could actually exist. While individual parts of them make sense, they just wouldn't work when they are put together as a whole object.

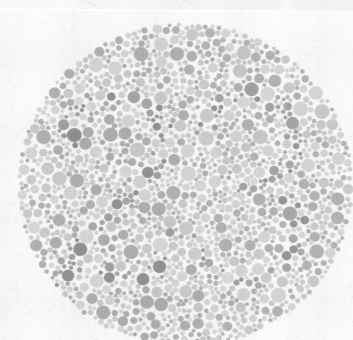

COLOUR VISION

Different cone cells in the retina detect different colours of light – red, blue or green. The levels of each of these is combined by the brain to create all the colours of the rainbow. However, some people are colour blind and they are unable to spot the difference between certain colours, such as red and green. Other people, known as tetrachromats, have cone cells that can detect four different colours, allowing them to detect even more colours.

Unless you are colour blind, you should be able to spot the number 23 made out of the dots in this picture.

MOVING PICTURES

Some single images can create the feeling of movement by using patterns that switch the light-sensitive cells on and off very quickly, tricking the brain into thinking it is moving. Movies and TV images create the illusion of movement by rapidly running a sequence of still pictures, called frames, on a screen in front of us. Movies and streaming video content use a frame rate of 24 frames per second (fps), while some high definition and slow-motion movies use frame rates of 48 fps or even up to 300 fps.

The sequence of still images shows a horse and rider. However if they were played in sequence and quite quickly, it would look as if the rider and horse are moving and jumping.

HEARING

The outer ears that sit on either side of your head are the visible body parts involved in hearing and they lead into the skull where the sound-sensitive organs lie.

INSIDE THE EAR

Sound waves are channelled into the ear by the outer ear flaps. They pass along the ear canal before hitting the eardrum, causing it to vibrate. This makes three tiny bones, called ossicles, move back and forth, pushing against a thin membrane at the opening to the cochlea. This causes vibrations to pass through the fluid inside the spiral of the cochlea and these make tiny hairs wave back and forth, triggering nerve signals that are sent to the brain.

HIGH AND LOW

The pitch of a sound is how high or low it is and it depends on the sound's frequency (the number of times the sound wave vibrates each second). It is measured in hertz (Hz). Humans can usually detect sounds that range from about 20 Hz to about 20,000 Hz.

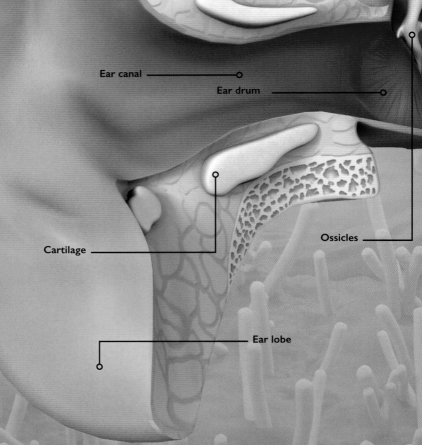

Skull bone

Ear canal

Ear drum

Ossicles

Cartilage

Ear lobe

Ear flap (pinna)

HOW LOUD?

The volume of sound is measured using decibels – the higher the number of decibels, the louder the sound is. A measurement of 0 decibels is the quietest sound we can hear, while 20 decibels is the noise made by leaves rustling. A sound with 130 decibels is the threshold of pain, while a jet engine from just 25 metres away will produce about 140 decibels.

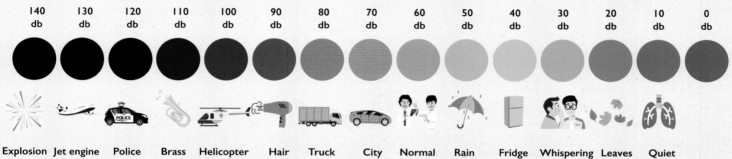

140 db	130 db	120 db	110 db	100 db	90 db	80 db	70 db	60 db	50 db	40 db	30 db	20 db	10 db	0 db
Explosion	Jet engine	Police siren	Brass band	Helicopter	Hair dryer	Truck	City traffic	Normal talking	Rain falling	Fridge humming	Whispering	Leaves rustling	Quiet breathing	

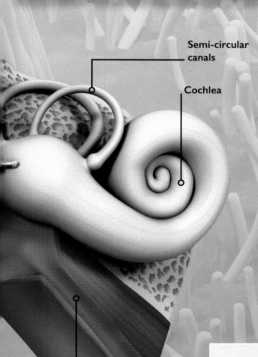

Semi-circular canals

Cochlea

Eustachian tube leads to the throat.

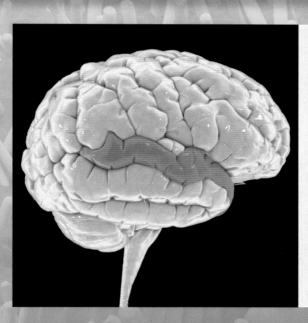

THE HEARING CENTRE

Signals from the cochlea travel along nerves to a part of the brain called the auditory cortex, which is part of the temporal lobes. Here the signals are interpreted as sounds. The auditory cortex is able to detect which direction a sound comes from, as it will reach one ear about 1/500th of a second before the other ear and will be very slightly louder.

PROTECTING YOUR HEARING

Your ears are very sensitive and can be easily damaged by loud sounds. It's important that you wear ear protection if you're in a noisy place for a long time and that you don't play music too loudly through headphones. People who have impaired hearing can use hearing aids or cochlea implants to help them to hear.

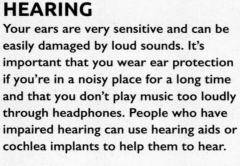

97

TASTE

Chemicals in your food can trigger your sense of taste, revealing a world of thousands of different flavours. The surface of the tongue, as well as the roof of the mouth and parts of the throat and epiglottis, are covered with tiny flavour receptors called taste buds.

This close-up image of the tongue shows how its surface is covered in bumps called papillae.

TASTE BUDS

Flavour particles in your food dissolve in water in your mouth and settle on the taste buds. This triggers signals that pass along nerves to the gustatory cortex, which is found in two places in the brain. This cross-section shows the taste buds on the tongue.

Pointed bumps are called filiform papillae.

Large round bumps are called circumvallate papillae.

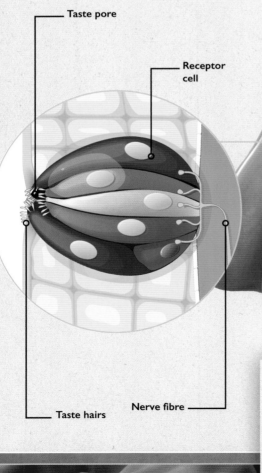

Taste pore

Receptor cell

Taste hairs

Nerve fibre

Taste buds

Nerve fibres

Muscle layer

Cross-section of the tongue showing the taste buds, muscles and nerves.

98

FLAVOURS

Your taste buds can detect five basic flavours, which mix together to form the different flavours of your food. These basic flavours are:

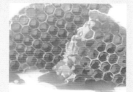    

SWEET
– from foods that are high in sugar, such as sweets, fruit and honey.

SOUR
– an acid flavour made by foods such as vinegar and lemons.

SALTY
– from foods that are high in salt, such as soy sauce, crisps and bacon.

BITTER
– made by foods such as coffee.

UMAMI
– a meaty flavour that comes from foods such as meat, cheese and mushrooms.

TASTE RECEPTORS

There are about 10,000 taste buds located on your tongue and around your mouth. However, your sense of taste is also affected by your sense of smell, which is why food can taste bland if you have a cold.

PROTECTING THE BODY

As well as helping you to enjoy your food, your sense of taste can also protect your body from harm. Many dangerous substances have a nasty bitter or sharp flavour to them, making them unpleasant to taste. You can then spit them out before they can cause any damage.

SMELL

Your sense of smell helps you to detect odours and scents from the world around you, whether they are the pleasant fragrances of flowers, the delicious aroma of some tasty food, or the nasty pong of something that could be harmful.

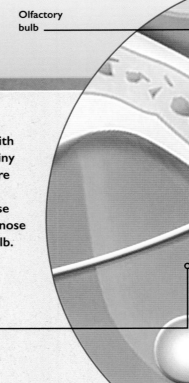

Olfactory signals sent into brain

INSIDE THE NOSE

When you take a good sniff, you are pulling air in through your nose and up into the roof of the nasal cavity that sits inside your skull. Here, scent particles dissolve into a mucus-like liquid that covers the roof of the nasal cavity.

SMELL CENTRE

Nerve signals pass from the olfactory bulb to a part of the brain called the primary olfactory cortex, which is found in the uncus located in the middle of the brain and neighbouring parts of the temporal lobe. Here the signals are interpreted and the scent is 'smelled'.

SMELLS EVERYWHERE

An adult can detect and spot the difference between up to 10,000 different odours. But while an adult human has about 25 million receptor cells in the nose, a hunting dog has about 220 million!

Olfactory bulb

SMELL RECEPTORS

The roof of the nasal cavity is covered with receptor cells, each of which ends with tiny hair-like cilia. Dissolved scent particles are trapped by these cilia and trigger the receptor cells to send nerve signals. These signals travel up through the roof of the nose and into an organ called the olfactory bulb.

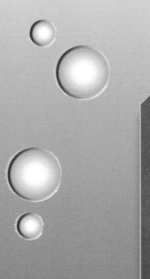

Nasal cavity

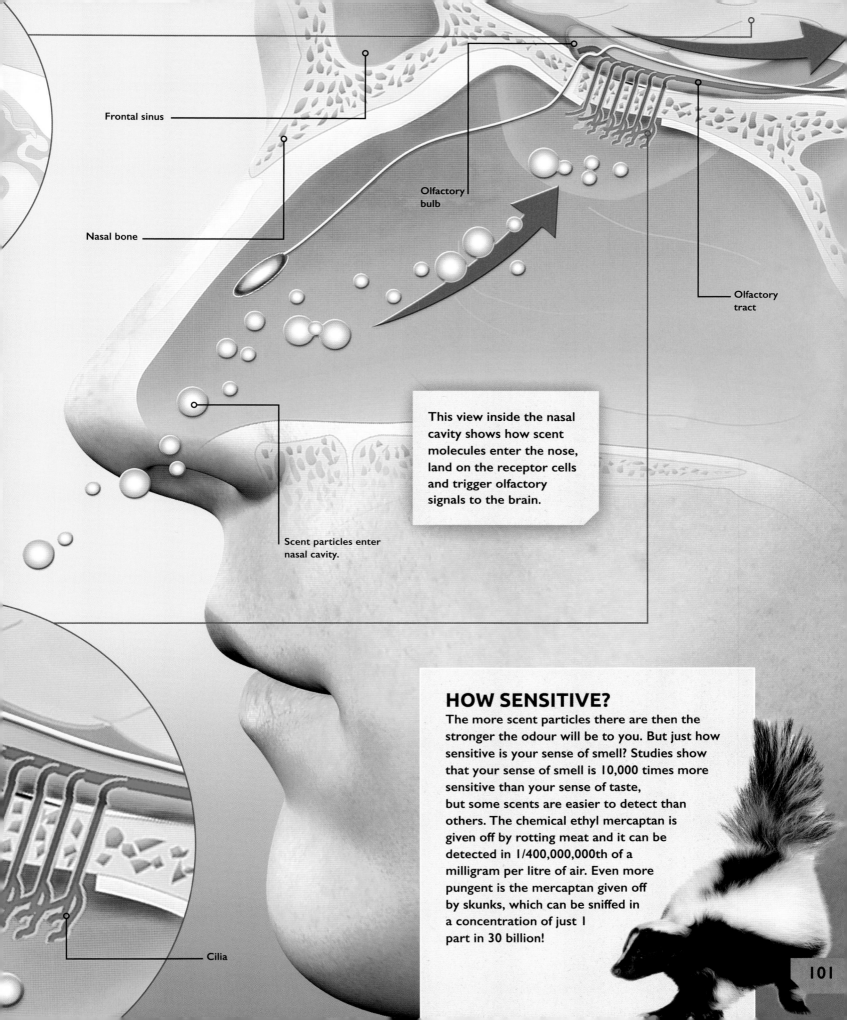

Frontal sinus

Nasal bone

Olfactory bulb

Olfactory tract

Scent particles enter nasal cavity.

This view inside the nasal cavity shows how scent molecules enter the nose, land on the receptor cells and trigger olfactory signals to the brain.

Cilia

HOW SENSITIVE?

The more scent particles there are then the stronger the odour will be to you. But just how sensitive is your sense of smell? Studies show that your sense of smell is 10,000 times more sensitive than your sense of taste, but some scents are easier to detect than others. The chemical ethyl mercaptan is given off by rotting meat and it can be detected in 1/400,000,000th of a milligram per litre of air. Even more pungent is the mercaptan given off by skunks, which can be sniffed in a concentration of just 1 part in 30 billion!

TOUCH AND PAIN

Your skin is packed with millions of different sense receptors that detect different sensations, including the light touch of a tickling feather, the heavier pressure of someone pushing you, or the painful prick of something sharp and dangerous.

SENSITIVE TOUCH

The human sense of touch is so sensitive that it can detect the difference in the height of two surfaces if they differ by just a single layer of molecules.

UNDER THE SKIN

The touch sense receptors are located in the dermis layer of the skin (see pages 10–11). These receptors include:

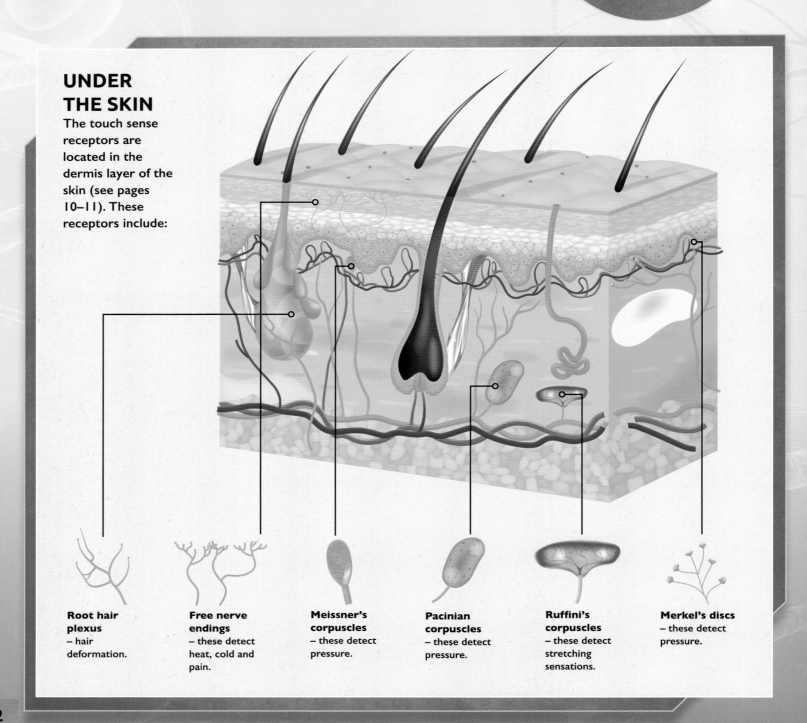

Root hair plexus – hair deformation.

Free nerve endings – these detect heat, cold and pain.

Meissner's corpuscles – these detect pressure.

Pacinian corpuscles – these detect pressure.

Ruffini's corpuscles – these detect stretching sensations.

Merkel's discs – these detect pressure.

PAIN

You may not like it, but sensing pain is a very useful way for your body to protect itself. Coming into contact with something hot or sharp can trigger a reflex reaction (see pages 82–83) and pull the affected part away from the source of pain before it can do too much damage. Body parts that have already been damaged will feel sore and painful for a while. This makes touching them unpleasant, so you leave them alone, allowing them to heal more quickly.

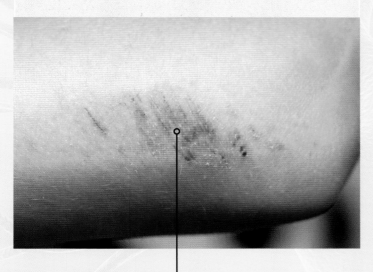

This scrape will feel sore, stopping you from touching it so that it can heal more quickly.

TOUCHY FEELY

Some parts of the body have more touch sense receptors than others, making them more sensitive. These body parts are either delicate and need more protection, or they are involved in touching and detecting the world around you. For example, the tips of the fingers are packed with far more touch receptors than the skin on your back.

SENSORY CORTEX

Touch sensations are sent to a thin strip of the brain called the sensory cortex. Parts of this strip deal with certain parts of the body and more-sensitive areas have a larger area than less-sensitive areas.

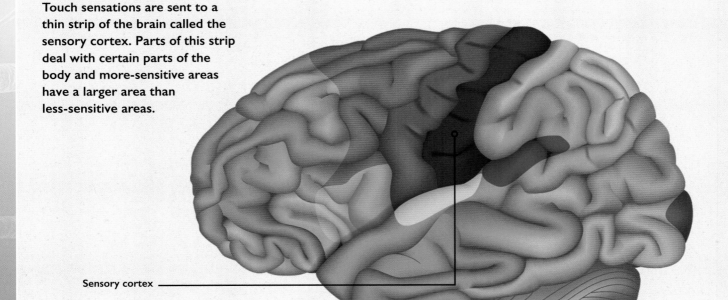

Sensory cortex

BALANCE AND OTHER SENSES

Have you ever tried standing on one leg – it's tricky, but not impossible. Special balance sensors inside your head will tell you if you're wobbling slightly so that your muscles can adjust and keep you upright.

LOTS OF SENSES

Scientists list many other senses beyond the five basic senses of touch, smell, taste, hearing and vision. These include all of the different senses that detect what's going on inside your body.

THE INNER EAR

Next to the cochlea in each ear are three fluid-filled tubes, called semicircular canals, which are set at right angles to each other. As your head moves, the fluid moves inside the tubes, and this movement is detected by sensitive cells. These send signals to the brain, telling it which way is up and how the body is moving in relation to that.

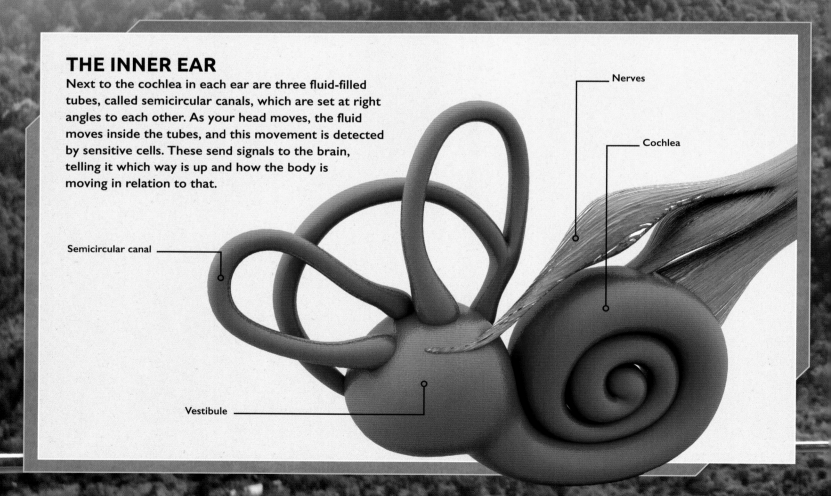

Nerves

Cochlea

Semicircular canal

Vestibule

PROPRIOCEPTION

Your sense of balance is helped by lots of other sensors located around the body. These are called proprioceptors and they are found in your muscles, tendons and joints. They send signals to your brain telling it where your body parts are, without you actually seeing them.

FEELING SEASICK

If the movement signals sent to your brain by your inner ear don't match what you can see, then you can start to feel a little bit sick. For example, staying inside a boat that is continually moving can make you feel nauseous because you can't see what's happening outside – this can be stopped by watching the horizon so that the signals sent by your eyes match those of your inner ear.

SPINNING AROUND

Spinning around very quickly causes the fluid in your inner ear to slosh about, and it takes time to stop moving around, even if you have. As a result, your brain receives a lot of confusing signals, making you feel dizzy. Dancers and ice skaters who have to spin very quickly, learn to keep their heads looking one way for as long as possible to reduce the amount of sloshing about by the inner ear fluid.

THE ENDOCRINE SYSTEM

Nerve signals aren't the only method your body uses to control different parts. It also has a collection of organs and glands that produce special chemicals called hormones that are carried around the body in the blood. These hormones take longer to act than nerve signals, but they still have a huge effect on your body.

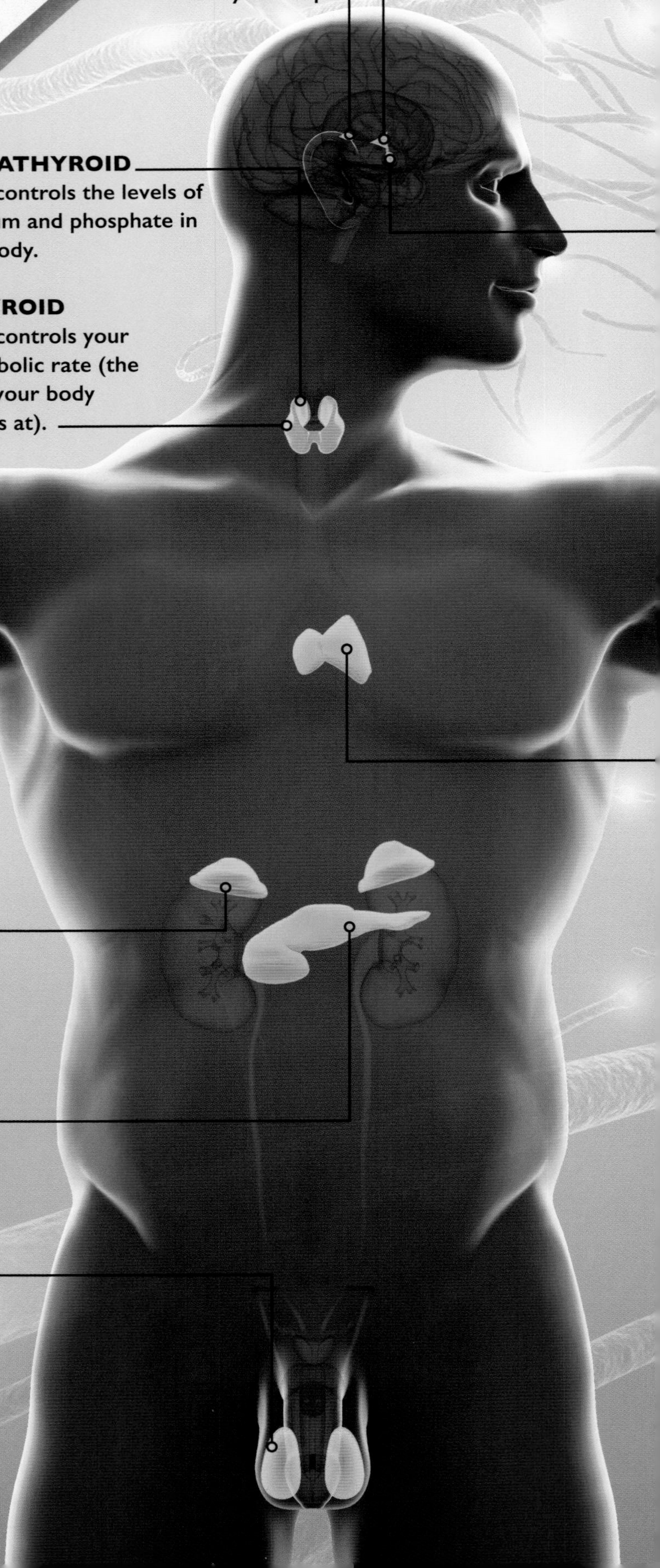

GLANDS AND HORMONES

The organs and glands that produce hormones collectively form the endocrine system. They are located in various places around the brain and torso.

PINEAL
This affects how you sleep.

PARATHYROID
This controls the levels of calcium and phosphate in the body.

THYROID
This controls your metabolic rate (the rate your body works at).

ADRENAL GLANDS
These affect your metabolism and blood pressure, as well as levels of potassium and sodium in the body.

PANCREAS
This controls the levels of sugar in the blood.

SEX ORGANS
Male sex organs, or testes (shown here), produce the male sex cells (sperm) and sex hormones, while the female sex organs, or ovaries produce the female sex cells (ova) and sex hormones (see pages 136–139).

HYPOTHALAMUS
This controls the release of some of the hormones from the pituitary gland.

PITUITARY
This produces several hormones that control growth as well as the actions of other glands in the endocrine system.

THYMUS
This helps to process certain types of immune cells.

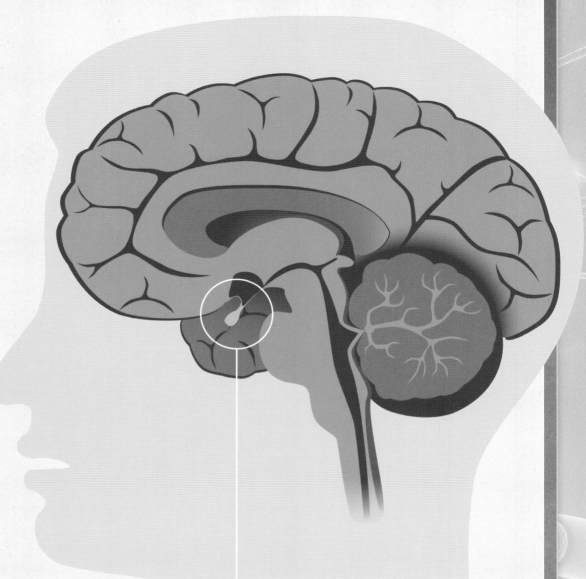

Hypothalamus

Anterior pituitary

Infundibular stalk

Posterior pituitary

THE MASTER GLAND
Located inside the brain, the pituitary gland is sometimes called the 'master gland'. The hormones it produces control the actions of many other endocrine glands around the body, affecting growth, blood pressure, body chemistry, stress levels, water levels, the production of milk in new mothers and the female sex hormones.

FIGHT OR FLIGHT?

Not all hormone reactions are slow-acting. For example, if you suddenly see something scary that could be dangerous, then parts of your body quickly leap into action, producing hormones that prepare you to confront the danger (fight) or run away (flight).

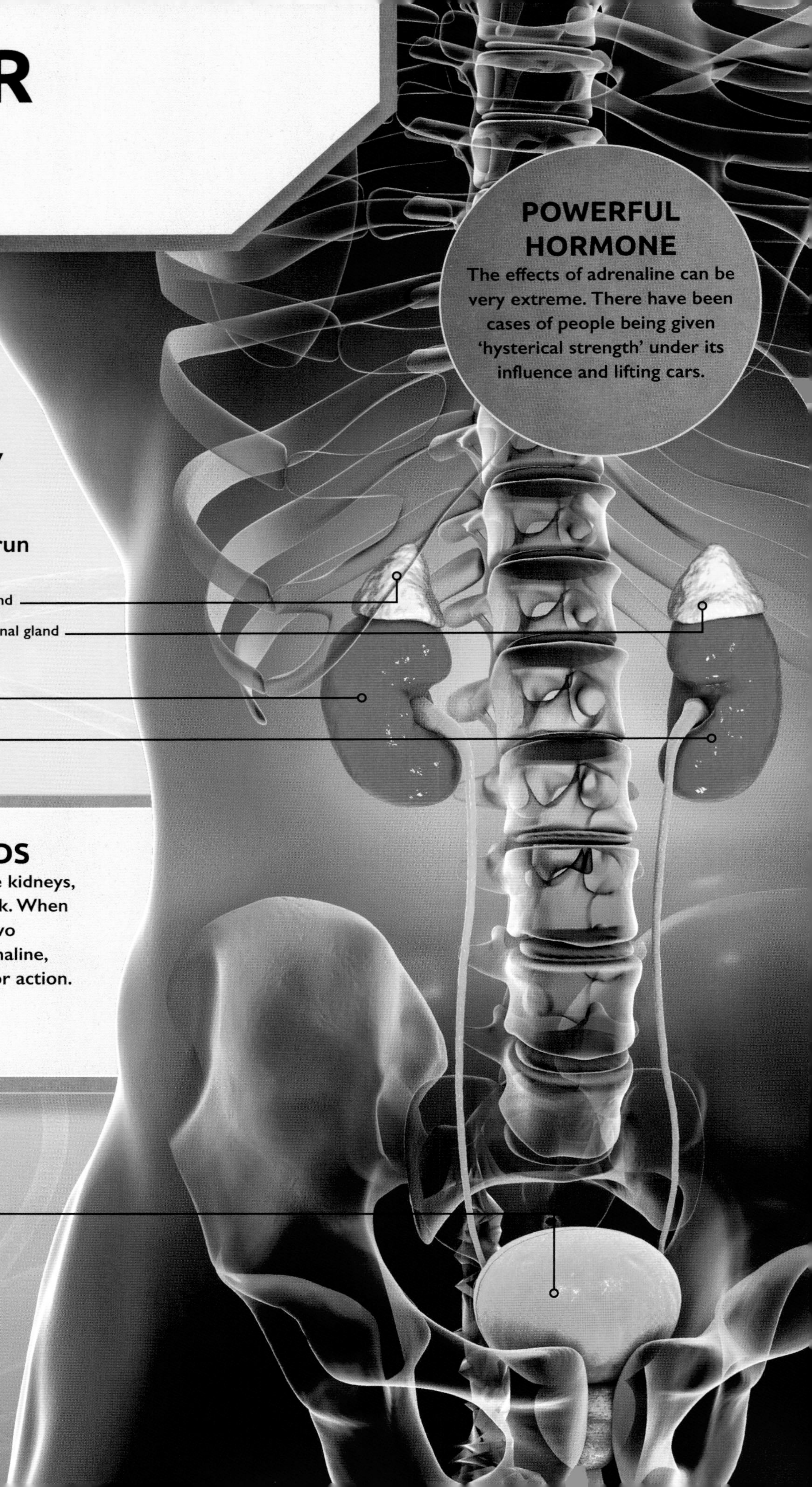

Left adrenal gland

Right adrenal gland

Left kidney

Right kidney

Bladder

POWERFUL HORMONE
The effects of adrenaline can be very extreme. There have been cases of people being given 'hysterical strength' under its influence and lifting cars.

THE ADRENAL GLANDS
The adrenal glands sit on top of the kidneys, which lie on either side of your back. When they are stimulated, they release two hormones, adrenaline and noradrenaline, both of which prepare your body for action.

PRIMED FOR ACTION

When adrenaline and noradrenaline enter the blood system, they produce a number of effects very quickly.

Some blood vessels get narrower (constrict) while others get larger (dilate), diverting blood and the oxygen and nutrients it carries to where they are needed most.

Digestion, a process that uses energy, is stopped temporarily.

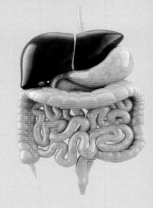

Blood flow to the muscles increases.

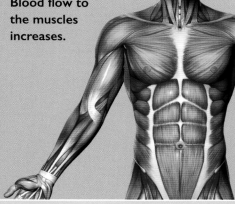

Your heart rate increases and your blood pressure rises.

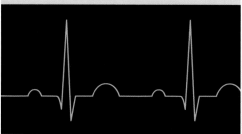

Your breathing rate increases to get more oxygen into your body.

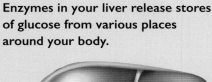

Your pupils widen so you see better.

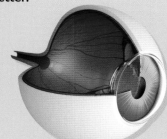

You sweat more to help cool your body while it is active.

Enzymes in your liver release stores of glucose from various places around your body.

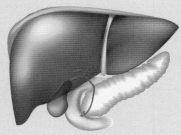

CALMING DOWN

The effects of adrenaline and noradrenaline are very short – the liver can process and make adrenaline inactive in just 3 minutes. Your body also produces another hormone in response to stress – cortisol. This helps your body use carbohydrates, proteins and fats more quickly, which, in turn, helps to reduce the effects of stress once the danger has passed.

CONTROLLING SUGAR

As well as being part of the digestive system (see pages 52–53), the pancreas has a role in the endocrine system. It secretes (produces and releases) hormones that help to control the levels of sugar in the blood.

THE PANCREAS

Inside the pancreas are special clusters of cells called islets of Langerhans. These produce the hormones glucagon and insulin, which are delivered straight into the bloodstream. There can be up to 2 million of these islets in the pancreas, but they only make up 1 per cent of the organ's weight.

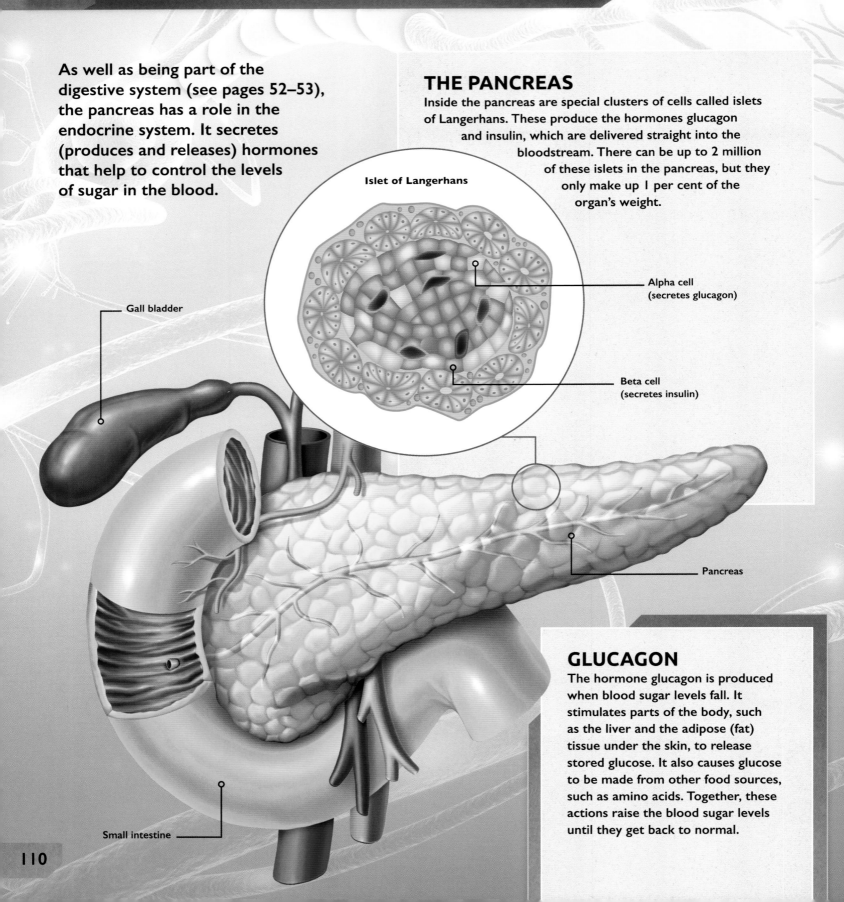

Islet of Langerhans

Alpha cell
(secretes glucagon)

Beta cell
(secretes insulin)

Gall bladder

Pancreas

Small intestine

GLUCAGON

The hormone glucagon is produced when blood sugar levels fall. It stimulates parts of the body, such as the liver and the adipose (fat) tissue under the skin, to release stored glucose. It also causes glucose to be made from other food sources, such as amino acids. Together, these actions raise the blood sugar levels until they get back to normal.

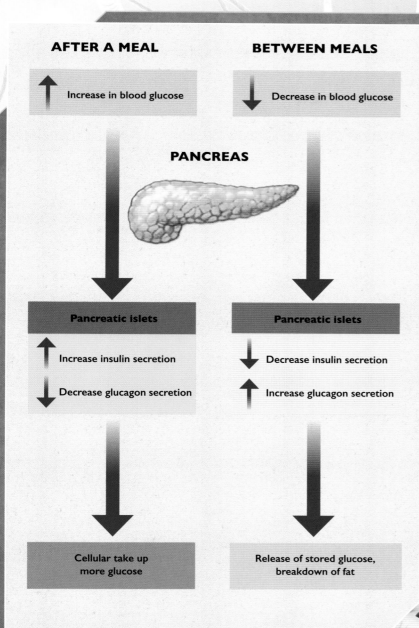

AFTER A MEAL

↑ Increase in blood glucose

BETWEEN MEALS

↓ Decrease in blood glucose

PANCREAS

Pancreatic islets

↑ Increase insulin secretion

↓ Decrease glucagon secretion

Pancreatic islets

↓ Decrease insulin secretion

↑ Increase glucagon secretion

Cellular take up more glucose

Release of stored glucose, breakdown of fat

INSULIN

The hormone insulin is produced when blood sugar levels rise. It stimulates parts of the body to convert glucose into other chemicals that the body can store, such as fatty acids and glycogen, and restricts the conversion of other food sources into glucose. In doing so, insulin reduces blood sugar levels until they get back to normal. Insulin and glucagon work together to maintain normal levels of glucose in the blood.

BLOOD SUGAR PROBLEMS

Diabetes is a condition in which levels of sugar in the blood can become too high. There are two types of diabetes:

TYPE 1 DIABETES

This is when the body's immune system destroys the cells that produce insulin, allowing blood sugar levels to increase.

TYPE 2 DIABETES

This is when the body does not produce enough insulin or the body's cells do not react to the insulin it does produce.

Both types of diabetes can be controlled by taking doses of insulin. Type 2 diabetes can sometimes be controlled without extra insulin by following a controlled diet.

If blood sugar levels fall too low, a condition called hypoglycemia occurs. In the short-term, this can be controlled by having a sugary snack or drink and, in the long-term, by eating a carefully controlled diet.

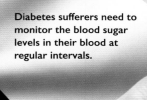

Diabetes sufferers need to monitor the blood sugar levels in their blood at regular intervals.

GROWTH HORMONE

During your childhood and teenage years, your body grows as bones get longer, muscles get bigger and organs grow larger. This increase in size is controlled by growth hormone.

THE PITUITARY GLAND

Growth hormone is one of the chemical messengers produced by the pituitary gland found at the base of the brain. Cells within the pituitary synthesise (produce) the hormone before it is released in the bloodstream.

Pituitary gland

Your pituitary gland is located at the base of your brain, just below your hypothalamus.

GROWTH HORMONE AT WORK

Growth hormone affects nearly every part of the body, causing muscle tissue to get bulkier, organs to grow larger and bones to get longer and thicker.

- It encourages parts of the body to increase the production of proteins, which helps with tissue growth, especially muscle tissue.

- It encourages the body to use its fat stores as an energy source.
- One of its main effects is to stimulate the liver to produce another hormone which encourages bones to grow longer and wider.

Levels of growth hormone are at their highest in the body during childhood, but especially during puberty (see pages 144–145), when sex hormones (see pages 136–139) stimulate the pituitary gland to produce even more growth hormone. This leads to a 'growth spurt' during teenage years, although the rate of growth can vary greatly from person to person. Growth hormone levels drop considerably when a person reaches adulthood and stops growing.

HOW BIG CAN WE GROW?

The amount that a person can grow depends on the levels of growth hormone they produce. If too much growth hormone is produced, then the person can grow very tall, leading to a condition called gigantism. The tallest person ever was American Robert Wadlow, who grew to a height of 2.72 metres (8 feet 11.1 inches). A lack of growth hormone will slow down bone growth and cause a condition called dwarfism, where the person is shorter than usual.

Robert Wadlow shown standing next to his father

PROTECTION

DEFENDING THE BODY

Your body is under attack all the time, whether it's from injuries caused by a knock or a fall or from microscopic bacteria or viruses. Fortunately, your body has a range of mechanisms it can use to repair any damage and to stop invaders from getting into the body.

Should any harmful microorganisms actually get inside your body, white blood cells can identify and destroy them before they can do any serious damage. These parts will also remember any new attackers so that your immune system is ready to fight them off should they try to invade again.

And if your body's defences fail, there is always medicine to fall back on. This can involve taking drugs to fight or prevent illnesses or, in more extreme cases, surgery to repair damaged body parts or even replace them completely!

Viruses, such as these HIV viruses, are a type of microorganism that need to use the cells of another living organism to multiply. In doing so, they can destroy the cell and, if enough get into a body, they can cause disease.

BARRIERS

The first barrier that any microorganisms face is the outside of your body, and some internal surfaces such as the lining of your gut.

As this photograph shows, a cough can expel around 3000 droplets at up to 80 kph (50 mph). A sneeze can throw out up to 100,000 droplets at speeds of about 160 kph (100 mph).

THE SKIN BARRIER

Your skin provides an outer protective barrier to your body that is tough to get through, unless it's been punctured by a wound. Its surface is covered with a thin layer of sebum, produced by the sebaceous glands (see pages 10–11). This liquid helps to keep skin and hair supple and also supports millions of friendly bacteria that live on your skin. These friendly bacteria help to protect you from any potentially harmful bacteria.

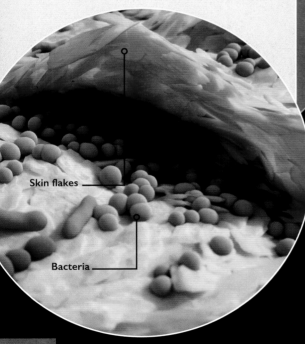

Skin flakes

Bacteria

COUGHS AND SNEEZES

The insides of your nose and throat are always coming into contact with microorganisms with every breath you take. However, if something irritates the linings of your nose and throat, it can cause you to either sneeze or cough the offending material out of your body.

VOMITING

If you eat something potentially harmful, it can make you feel nauseous and, if the feeling is strong enough, it could even make you sick. Powerful muscle contractions in the stomach push its contents back up through the oesophagus and into the mouth to be vomited out.

MUCUS

Many of the surface linings inside the body are covered with sticky mucus, including the nose, throat and oesophagus. This can trap dust, dirt and germs that can be sneezed or coughed out or swallowed and destroyed by the powerful acids in the stomach (see pages 48–49).

FEVER

If germs do get into your body and infect it, your body may respond by producing a fever, raising your body temperature above its normal level of 37°C (98.6°F). The higher temperature reduces the rate at which germs multiply and also helps your body's own infection-fighting cells.

TEARS

Tear glands above your eyes regularly produce tears to keep the front of your eyes moist. If dust or other particles get into your eyes, the irritation stimulates the tear ducts to produce more tears to wash away the irritant. Tears also contain chemicals that can attack and destroy some bacteria.

BLOOD CLOTTING

Even a small wound can result in bleeding and, if the blood loss isn't stopped in time, then the results could be dangerous. Your blood contains platelets and chemicals that can produce blood clots to plug a wound and stop the leak.

STAGES OF WOUND HEALING

When a wound forms, the muscles in the walls of the blood vessels contract to make the blood vessels narrower. This reduces the flow of blood to the area and limits blood loss. This is called vasoconstriction.

Platelets are small fragments of cells made in our bone marrow. The platelets become sticky when they come into contact with body tissues outside the blood vessels. The platelets start to clump together to form a plug.

If this doesn't stop the wound, then strands of a substance called fibrin are produced.

These strands create a net of fibres that can trap red blood cells. The net starts to contract, squeezing the trapped blood cells and hardening them to form a solid blood clot to cover the wound.

Red blood cells

KEEPING IT MOVING

Blood clots don't usually form in your blood because the enzymes that produce a clot aren't released until the platelets start to clump together.

Fibrin

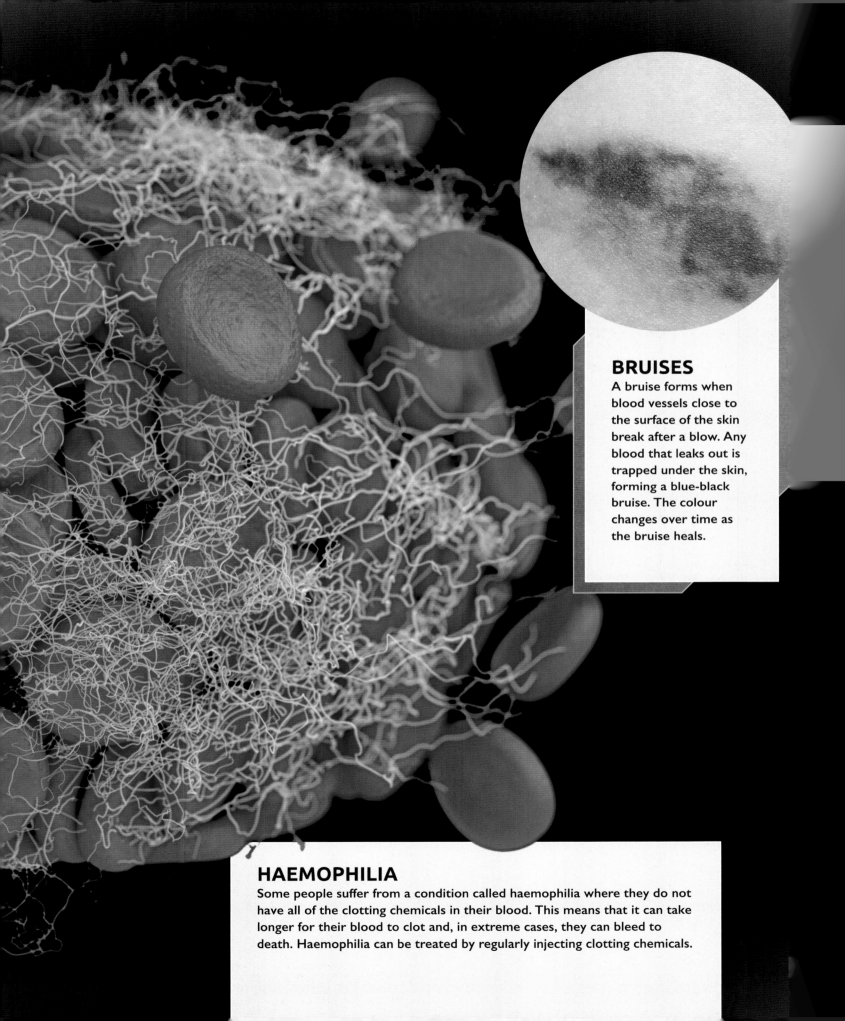

BRUISES

A bruise forms when blood vessels close to the surface of the skin break after a blow. Any blood that leaks out is trapped under the skin, forming a blue-black bruise. The colour changes over time as the bruise heals.

HAEMOPHILIA

Some people suffer from a condition called haemophilia where they do not have all of the clotting chemicals in their blood. This means that it can take longer for their blood to clot and, in extreme cases, they can bleed to death. Haemophilia can be treated by regularly injecting clotting chemicals.

LYMPHATIC SYSTEM

The body's cells are surrounded by a special fluid. The lymphatic system acts as a drain, carrying away the lymph fluid. This fluid enters into tiny lymphatic capillaries, which join to form larger vessels that pass through small swellings called lymph nodes, where any harmful pathogens are attacked and destroyed.

Lymph nodes

Lymphatic vessels

WHAT'S IN LYMPH?
An adult body will have up to 2 litres (3.5 pints) of lymph fluid flowing around it. This fluid is similar to blood, but it doesn't contain the red blood cells or some of the proteins. It does contain white blood cells which attack any pathogens that get into the lymph. This fluid leaks out of blood vessels and bathes the body's cells.

MOVING LYMPH
Once it has entered the lymphatic capillaries, lymph flows into larger and larger lymphatic vessels that eventually empty the lymph fluid into the veins that are just above the heart. Unlike the circulatory system, where the heart pushes blood around the body, the lymphatic system has no central pump and empties the fluid it carries into veins just above the heart.

Excess fluid enters the lymphatic capillary.

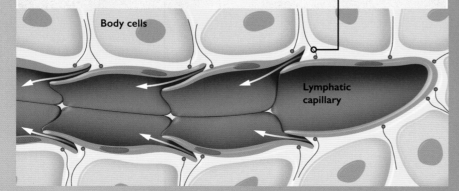

Body cells

Lymphatic capillary

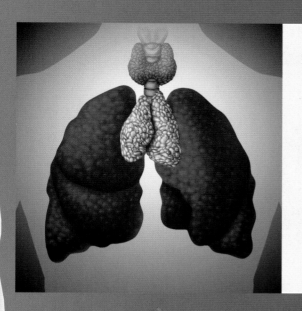

THYMUS AND SPLEEN

The lymphatic system also has a couple of organs. The thymus (left), which is found in the chest, is where white blood cells called lymphocytes develop. The spleen (right) is on the left side of the body near the stomach. It helps to filter blood and mature some types of white blood cell.

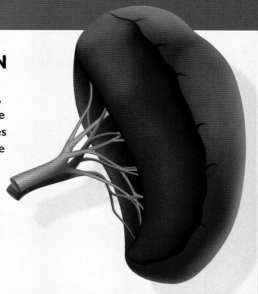

Lymphoid tissue containing white blood cells

Outgoing lymph vessel

Lymph node

Vein

Artery

Incoming lymph vessel

SWOLLEN NODES

When you get an infection, increased activity inside your lymph nodes causes them to swell. You can feel these swollen nodes by touching the cluster of nodes located just behind your jaw and beneath your ears.

LYMPH NODES

Scattered along the lymphatic system are small, bean-shaped swellings, called lymph nodes, that can be up to 2.5 cm long. These nodes filter harmful pathogens out of the lymph fluid. They also store white blood cells that can attack these pathogens and destroy them.

MOVING LYMPH AROUND

The lymphatic system doesn't have a pump, like the circulatory system. Instead, lymph is pushed around the system when your body movements squeeze the lymphatic vessels. Inside the vessels are valves that stop the fluid from flowing the wrong way.

WHITE BLOOD CELLS

White blood cells are also known as leukocytes. They are larger than red blood cells, but they can change shape to squeeze out of blood vessels to patrol your body's cells and tissues. Their job is to destroy any pathogens and clean up dead cells and damaged tissue.

White blood cell

TYPES OF WHITE BLOOD CELLS

There are several different types of white blood cell and, unlike red blood cells, they all have a cell nucleus. They are made in the bone marrow (see pages 18–19) and mature inside the nodes of the lymphatic system (see pages 120–121). Normally, there are between 4,000 and 11,000 white blood cells in every cubic millimetre of blood, but their numbers rise during an infection to as high as 25,000 per cubic millimetre.

NEUTROPHILS

These make up between 50–70 per cent of the white blood cells in your body. They destroy pathogens and swarm around cuts to combat infection. They also produce the yellowy substance called pus.

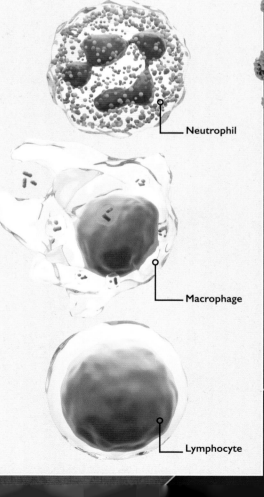

Neutrophil

MACROPHAGES

These white blood cells destroy pathogens in the bloodstream and clean up debris from damaged tissue around a wound.

Macrophage

LYMPHOCYTES

These white blood cells destroy pathogens in several different ways. Some can inject them with poison to kill them, while others produce special markers, called antibodies, which will stick to pathogens and attract other white blood cells to destroy the invaders.

Lymphocyte

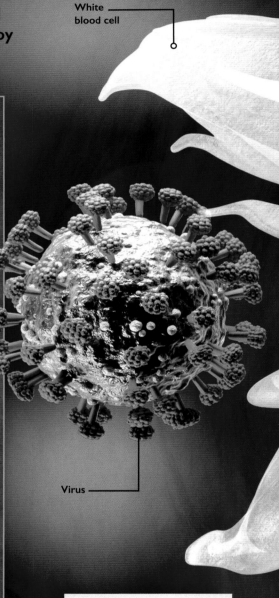

Virus

This image shows a white blood cell in the act of reaching out to envelop and destroy a virus by phagocytosis.

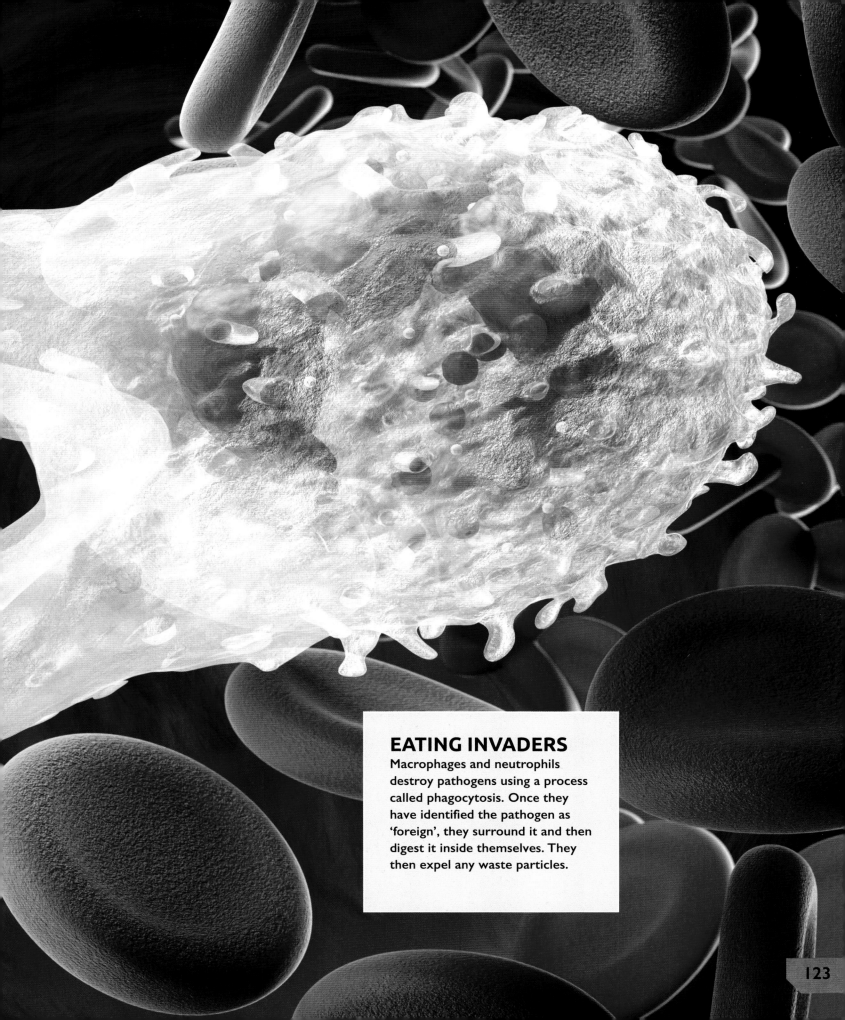

EATING INVADERS
Macrophages and neutrophils destroy pathogens using a process called phagocytosis. Once they have identified the pathogen as 'foreign', they surround it and then digest it inside themselves. They then expel any waste particles.

FIGHTING INFECTION

The majority of pathogens are stopped by your body's outer defences (see pages 116–117), however, a few may succeed in sneaking in. When this happens, it's your immune system's job to identify and destroy these pathogens before they can do any harm.

UNDER ATTACK

Your body is under attack from a wide range of pathogens. These include fungus, such as the fungi that causes athlete's foot, parasites, including tapeworms and Plasmodium which causes malaria, bacteria (such as the bacteria that cause food poisoning) and viruses such as the common cold and the SARS-CoV-2 virus, which causes COVID-19.

Antibody

ANTIBODIES

To identify the pathogen, your immune system uses special chemicals called antibodies, which are made by white blood cells and designed to attach to a specific pathogen. Other parts of your immune system can then spot the antibodies on these pathogens and attack them.

These antibodies have been released into the blood stream and are ready to attach to a pathogen.

MARKING INTRUDERS

When a pathogen enters your body, it multiplies and eventually some of it ends up in your lymphatic system, where it is carried to one of the lymph nodes. Inside the node, lots of different antibody cells rub against the pathogen until one of them identifies it and sticks to it. When this happens the antibody cell multiplies rapidly and these new cells produce lots of antibodies that enter the blood vessels and attached themselves to other pathogens.

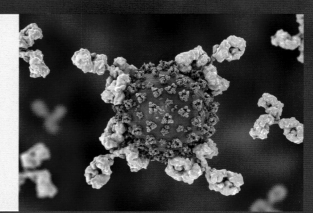

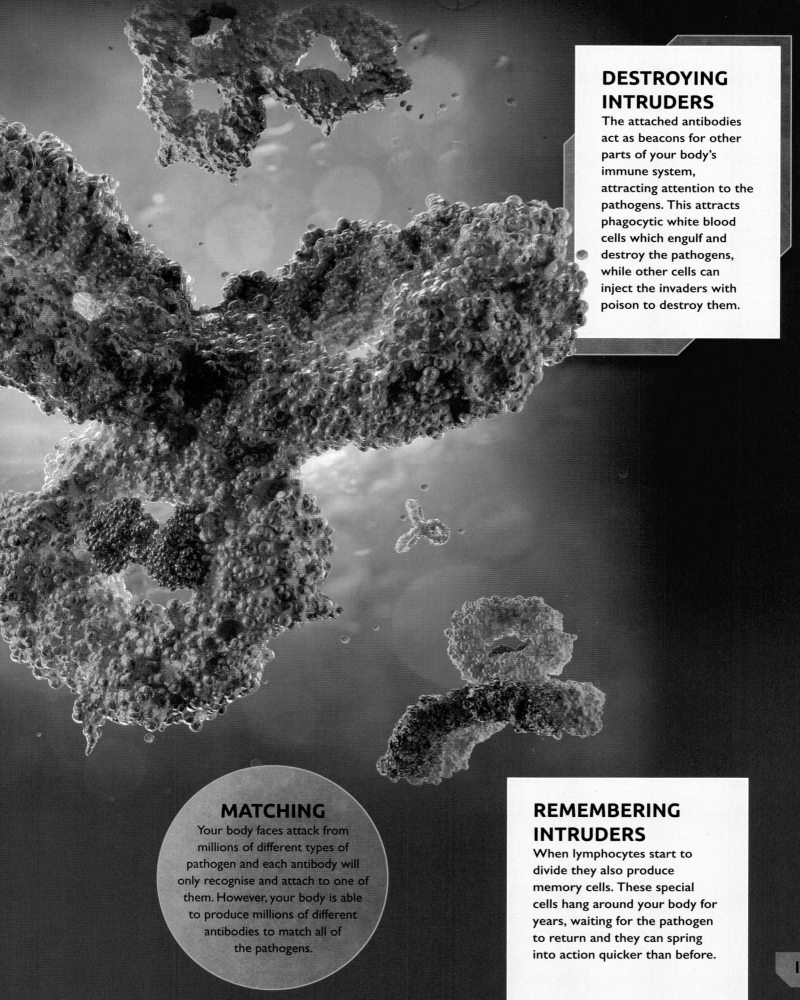

DESTROYING INTRUDERS

The attached antibodies act as beacons for other parts of your body's immune system, attracting attention to the pathogens. This attracts phagocytic white blood cells which engulf and destroy the pathogens, while other cells can inject the invaders with poison to destroy them.

MATCHING

Your body faces attack from millions of different types of pathogen and each antibody will only recognise and attach to one of them. However, your body is able to produce millions of different antibodies to match all of the pathogens.

REMEMBERING INTRUDERS

When lymphocytes start to divide they also produce memory cells. These special cells hang around your body for years, waiting for the pathogen to return and they can spring into action quicker than before.

ALLERGIC REACTIONS

While your immune system protects your body from attack, it can go too far in some people and attack harmless substances, causing a range of symptoms from a sniffly nose to serious life-threatening reactions. This over-reaction is called an allergy.

TRIGGERING REACTIONS

Substances that cause allergies are called allergens and they trigger a reaction when they are breathed in, swallowed or touched. Common triggers include pollen, nuts and insect stings. They can cause swelling and soreness.

This photo shows a plant releasing a cloud made up of millions of tiny pollen grains. Plants release their pollen mainly during the spring and summer months.

HISTAMINE

When some allergens enter the body, they attach themselves to antibodies on certain white blood cells. This causes the white blood cells to burst and release a chemical called histamine. Histamine, in turn, causes the body tissues nearby to become swollen and sore as if they have been infected.

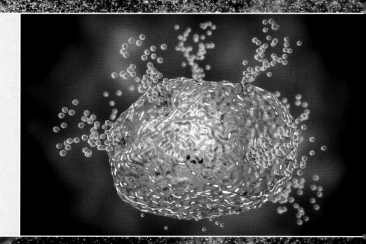

DIFFERENT ALLERGIES

Different allergens can trigger different responses. Pollen can irritate the tissues of the nose and mouth, causing the runny nose and streaming eyes of hay fever. Asthma is caused by allergens entering the airways, causing the airway to contract and produce lots of mucus, making breathing difficult. Some allergic reactions are very serious and can affect the whole body, even causing the heart to stop. This is called anaphylaxis and it can be triggered by insect stings or by eating eggs or nuts.

TESTING AND TREATING

Sometimes it can be hard to work out what is causing an allergic reaction, so doctors carry out skin tests, putting small amounts of different substances onto the skin to see which ones make the skin sore and red. They can then work out how to treat any symptoms the allergen causes.

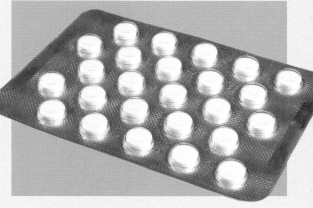

People with hayfever can take medicines called antihistamines, which counter the effects of the released histamine.

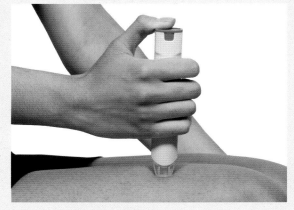

Asthma sufferers can use special inhalers, which release drugs into the airways to relax them and open them up.

People who could suffer anaphylaxis may need to carry doses of adrenaline that they inject into their bodies if they come into contact with an allergen. The adrenalin reduces the body's allergic response.

MEDICINE AND SURGERY

The earliest medical procedures were more about religious beliefs and philosophy than scientific research. Early medical treatments included using leeches to drain blood from a patient and trepanning, which involved drilling holes into the patient's skull. These treatments were rarely successful and, more often than not, they could prove dangerous to the patient.

MEDICAL ADVANCES
Over the years, people have studied the human body and tried to find out how it works and how to fix things when they go wrong. Here are some of the milestones:

C. 2600 BCE
The Egyptian Imhotep becomes one of the first known physicians and describes how to diagnose and treat some 200 diseases.

C. 130–216 CE
The Roman-Greek physician Galen creates several theories about how the body works, many of which were later shown to be wrong, but remained influential for about 1,500 years.

1543
Flemish physician Andreas Vesalius publishes *On the Structure of the Human Body*, which includes accurate descriptions of human anatomy.

1780
Italian physician Luigi Galvani carries out experiments using electricity, nerves and muscles.

1818
James Blundell performs the first successful human blood transfusion.

c.2600 BCE | 2ND CENTURY BCE | c.420 BCE | c.130–216 CE | c.1010 CE | 1543 | 1628 | 1670 | 1780 | 1796 | 1818

1628
English doctor William Harvey describes how blood circulates around the body.

1796
English doctor Edward Jenner develops a vaccination for smallpox.

2ND CENTURY BCE
Evidence of medicine using seeds and herbs from China's Shang Dynasty.

C. 420 BCE
The Greek doctor **Hippocrates**, later known as the 'father of modern medicine', creates the Hippocratic Oath for physicians, which is still used today.

C. 1010 CE
The Arab physician Ibn Sina, known as Avicenna, wrote *The Canon of Medicine*, which becomes a standard medical textbook.

C. 1670
Dutch scientist **Antonie von Leeuwenhoek** uses an early microscope to discover human cells, including red blood cells and sperm.

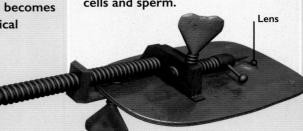

Lens

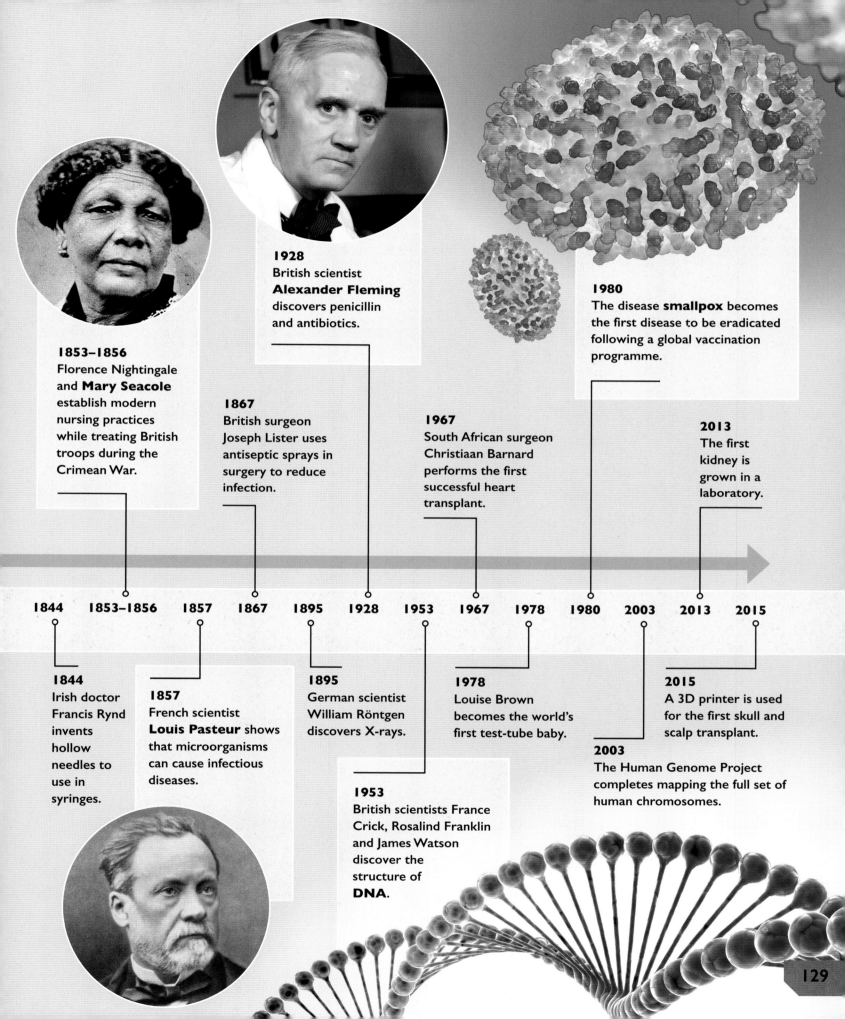

1928
British scientist **Alexander Fleming** discovers penicillin and antibiotics.

1980
The disease **smallpox** becomes the first disease to be eradicated following a global vaccination programme.

1853–1856
Florence Nightingale and **Mary Seacole** establish modern nursing practices while treating British troops during the Crimean War.

1867
British surgeon Joseph Lister uses antiseptic sprays in surgery to reduce infection.

1967
South African surgeon Christiaan Barnard performs the first successful heart transplant.

2013
The first kidney is grown in a laboratory.

1844   1853–1856   1857   1867   1895   1928   1953   1967   1978   1980   2003   2013   2015

1844
Irish doctor Francis Rynd invents hollow needles to use in syringes.

1857
French scientist **Louis Pasteur** shows that microorganisms can cause infectious diseases.

1895
German scientist William Röntgen discovers X-rays.

1978
Louise Brown becomes the world's first test-tube baby.

2015
A 3D printer is used for the first skull and scalp transplant.

2003
The Human Genome Project completes mapping the full set of human chromosomes.

1953
British scientists France Crick, Rosalind Franklin and James Watson discover the structure of **DNA**.

129

IMMUNISATION

Your immune system can be given a helping hand by vaccines. These medicines stimulate antibodies in the body that will help fight disease by recognising and destroying infected cells.

EARLY PROTECTION

Smallpox was a highly dangerous disease that caused fever, headaches and body sores and, in the 18th century, led to the deaths of as many as 30 per cent of the people it infected. Early methods of protecting against the disease included variolation, which exposed the patient to smallpox. For example, the practice of blowing powdered scabs from other smallpox sufferers up the patient's nose was used in China from the 15th century.

JENNER AND SMALLPOX

British doctor, Edward Jenner, developed the first vaccine for smallpox in 1796. Jenner developed his vaccine from the cowpox virus, a similar, but much less harmful virus, to trigger an immune response in people. Jenner's vaccine was safer than earlier attempts, because there was no chance of getting smallpox from it.

SAVING LIVES

According to the World Health Organization, vaccines save an estimated 2–3 million lives around the planet every single year.

A medic administers a vaccine by injection. Vaccines can be given through injections, by mouth or they can be sprayed into the roof of the nasal cavity.

HOW VACCINES WORK

There are several different types of vaccine. These include:

• Attenuated vaccines use a weakened form of the microorganisms that cause a disease. These microorganisms can no longer cause serious illness, but they can still trigger an immune response. Some can cause a mild form of the disease. Attenuated vaccines include those for measles, mumps, rubella and polio.

• Inactivated vaccines contain microorganisms that have been killed or inactivated using heat or chemicals. Even though they are harmless, they will still trigger an immune response. Inactivated vaccines include those against rabies, cholera and influenza.

• Subunit vaccines use proteins that are found on the outer surface of the harmful material. Subunit vaccines include those against tetanus, diphtheria and whooping cough.

• Some modern vaccines use genetic material from a harmful microorganism to stimulate the immune response to that organism.

SUCCESSFUL VACCINES

Vaccines have proved successful at cutting the rates of infection in many diseases and, as a result, have saved millions of lives. Smallpox is an extremely dangerous disease, but it has now been eradicated thanks to a global immunisation programme. Rates of polio cases have also plummeted, from 350,000 cases of wild poliovirus in 1988 to just 175 reported cases in 2019.

REPLACING BODY PARTS

Some worn out or damaged body parts can be replaced with artificial devices called protheses. While some prostheses are simply for cosmetic purposes, others are designed to recreate the function of the replaced body part.

OLD REPLACEMENTS

One of the oldest prostheses ever discovered was an artificial toe made from wood and leather. It was found on an ancient Egyptian mummy that was more than 2,700 years old.

ARTIFICIAL LIMBS

Some of the earliest replacement body parts included eye prosthetics made from bitumen paste and artificial limbs carved from wood and iron. Modern prostheses use the latest materials, such as carbon fibre and silicon, and 3D printing techniques to create lifelike replacements that can recreate the body part. Some prostheses are fitted with implants that connect directly to the wearer's nervous system, allowing them to control the device by thinking. They also have sensors that can send feedback to the wearer, allowing them to adjust their actions.

REPLACING INTERNAL PARTS

Internal organs can be replaced either with organs from donors, artificial organs and even body parts that have been grown from stem cells or artificially in a laboratory. Common organ transplants include kidneys, heart, bone marrow, lungs and liver, but other body parts that have been successfully replaced include arms, legs and faces. Smaller body parts can also be replaced, including heart valves and corneas in eyes.

SPORTING PROSTHESES

As well as creating lifelike replacements for body parts, specialist prostheses can allow people to take part in sporting events. These include lower leg prosthetics for runners and arm and hand prosthetics for weightlifters, golfers, baseball players and anglers.

BIRTH AND AGEING

THE CYCLE OF LIFE

Even though your body is made from trillions of cells, each of us starts out as just one, single cell, the product of fertilisation with special sex cells from a male and a female. During nine months, this single cell multiplies and develops before being born as a human baby.

Over the following years, this human grows, developing through childhood as limbs lengthen and body parts enlarge and mature. Puberty arrives during the teenage years, and the body undergoes a surge in growth towards its full size. During this time, the sex hormones start to be released, preparing the body for sexual maturity and reproduction.

Following the growth spurt of puberty, the body reaches maturity around the ages of 18–20. This is the start of adulthood and the body is at its peak and ready to reproduce.

After a period of maturity, the body then starts to age and certain abilities start to decline into old age. Worn out or damaged parts take longer to heal and repair, hair starts to thin and skin starts to wrinkle as it becomes less elastic. At the same time, muscles become weaker, joints stiffen and bones may become more brittle, while some of our senses, especially vision and hearing, will decline.

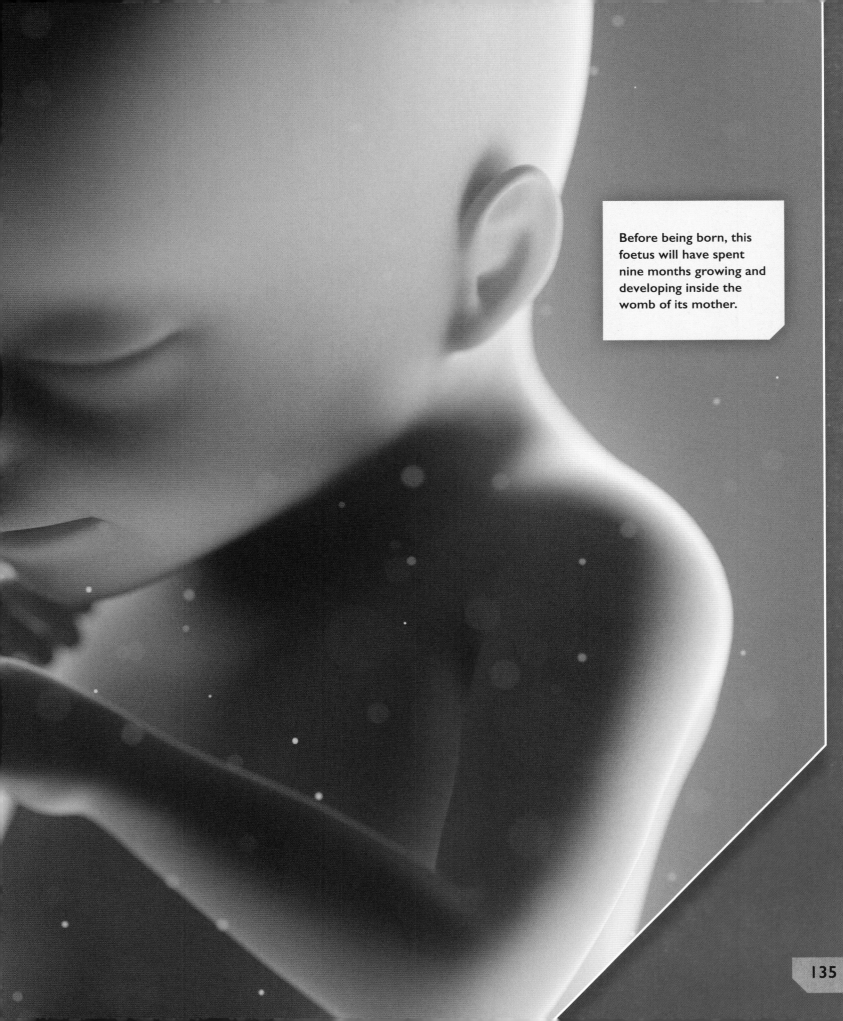

Before being born, this foetus will have spent nine months growing and developing inside the womb of its mother.

THE REPRODUCTIVE SYSTEMS

The purpose of the reproductive systems is to produce children that carry genetic information from both the mother and the father. This genetic information is carried in male sperm and female eggs and these are produced by the male and female reproductive systems.

Bladder

Seminal vesicle

Prostate gland

Vas deferens

Penis

Epididymis

Testis

MALE REPRODUCTIVE SYSTEM

The male reproductive system is made up of the two testes and the penis, which hang outside the male body. This keeps the testes a little cooler than body temperature, which is ideal for making sperm. During puberty, an increase in the production of the male sex hormone, testosterone, leads to an increase in sperm production by the testes.

SPERM

Sperm are the male sex cells and they store their genetic information inside the dome-shaped head. Behind this is a long tail, which the sperm beats vigorously as it swims towards the female egg.

Tail

Head

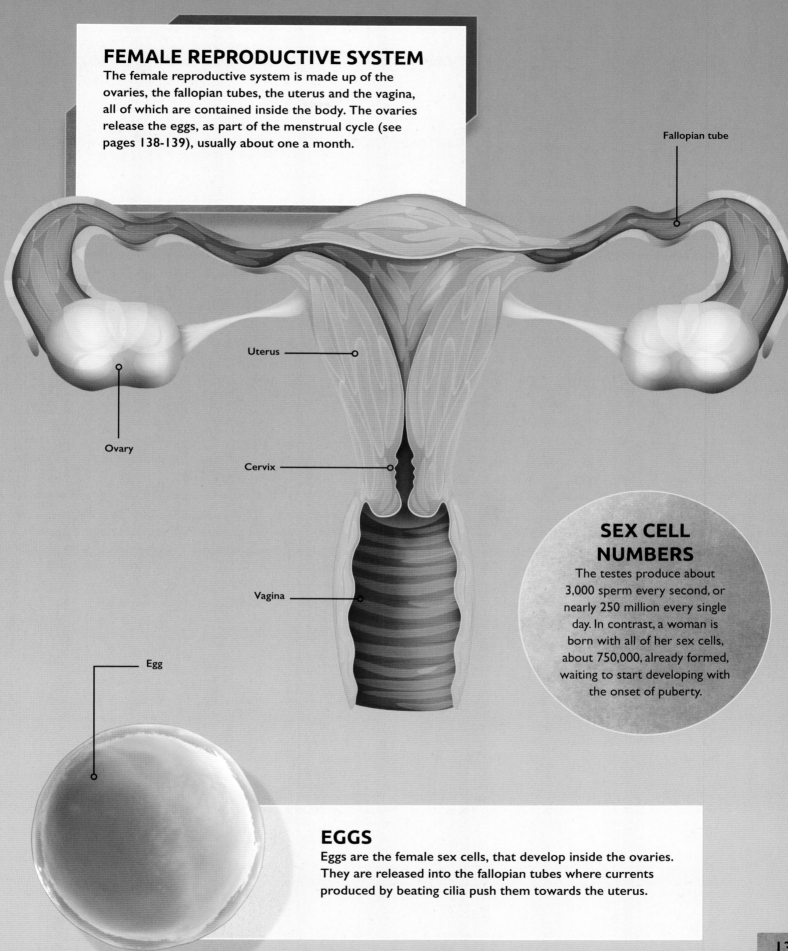

FEMALE REPRODUCTIVE SYSTEM

The female reproductive system is made up of the ovaries, the fallopian tubes, the uterus and the vagina, all of which are contained inside the body. The ovaries release the eggs, as part of the menstrual cycle (see pages 138-139), usually about one a month.

Fallopian tube

Uterus

Ovary

Cervix

Vagina

Egg

SEX CELL NUMBERS

The testes produce about 3,000 sperm every second, or nearly 250 million every single day. In contrast, a woman is born with all of her sex cells, about 750,000, already formed, waiting to start developing with the onset of puberty.

EGGS

Eggs are the female sex cells, that develop inside the ovaries. They are released into the fallopian tubes where currents produced by beating cilia push them towards the uterus.

THE MENSTRUAL CYCLE

While the male sex organs produce sperm all the time, the female sex organs release eggs on a 28-day cycle called the menstrual cycle. This is in response to the changing levels of hormones, such as oestrogen, progesterone, follicle-stimulating hormone and luteinizing hormone.

THE MENSTRUAL CYCLE

The menstrual cycle usually lasts for 28 days, but it can last as many as 40 or as few as 21. During this time, an egg is released from one of the ovaries (or sometimes two may be released at the same time) and the wall of the uterus builds up, in readiness to receive a fertilised egg (see pages 142–143).

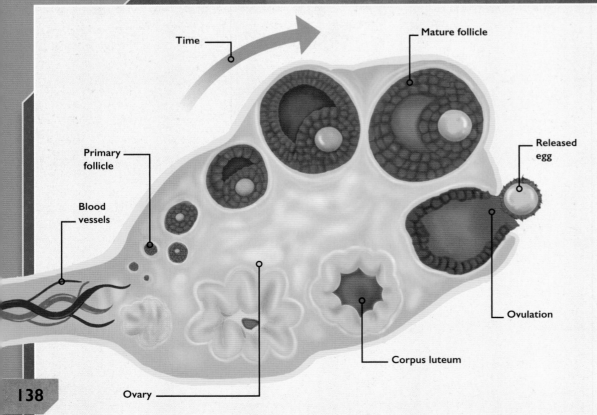

Time

Mature follicle

Primary follicle

Blood vessels

Released egg

Ovulation

Corpus luteum

Ovary

RELEASING AN EGG

For the first few days of the menstrual cycle, oocytes inside the ovaries start to mature and develop. Every month, between 100-150 will go through this process, but only one will usually reach maturity. Once full maturity has been reached, usually around the middle of the menstrual cycle, the egg is released from the ovary into one of the fallopian tubes to begin its journey to the uterus. The release of the egg from the ovary is called ovulation.

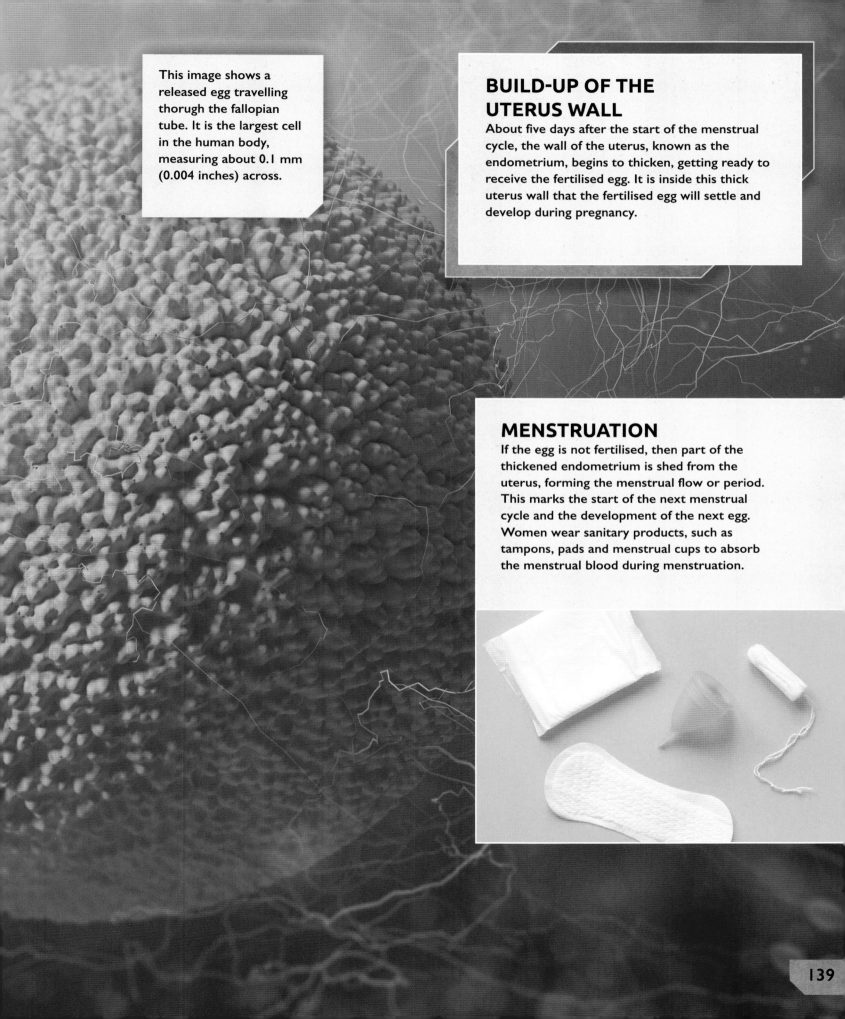

This image shows a released egg travelling thorugh the fallopian tube. It is the largest cell in the human body, measuring about 0.1 mm (0.004 inches) across.

BUILD-UP OF THE UTERUS WALL

About five days after the start of the menstrual cycle, the wall of the uterus, known as the endometrium, begins to thicken, getting ready to receive the fertilised egg. It is inside this thick uterus wall that the fertilised egg will settle and develop during pregnancy.

MENSTRUATION

If the egg is not fertilised, then part of the thickened endometrium is shed from the uterus, forming the menstrual flow or period. This marks the start of the next menstrual cycle and the development of the next egg. Women wear sanitary products, such as tampons, pads and menstrual cups to absorb the menstrual blood during menstruation.

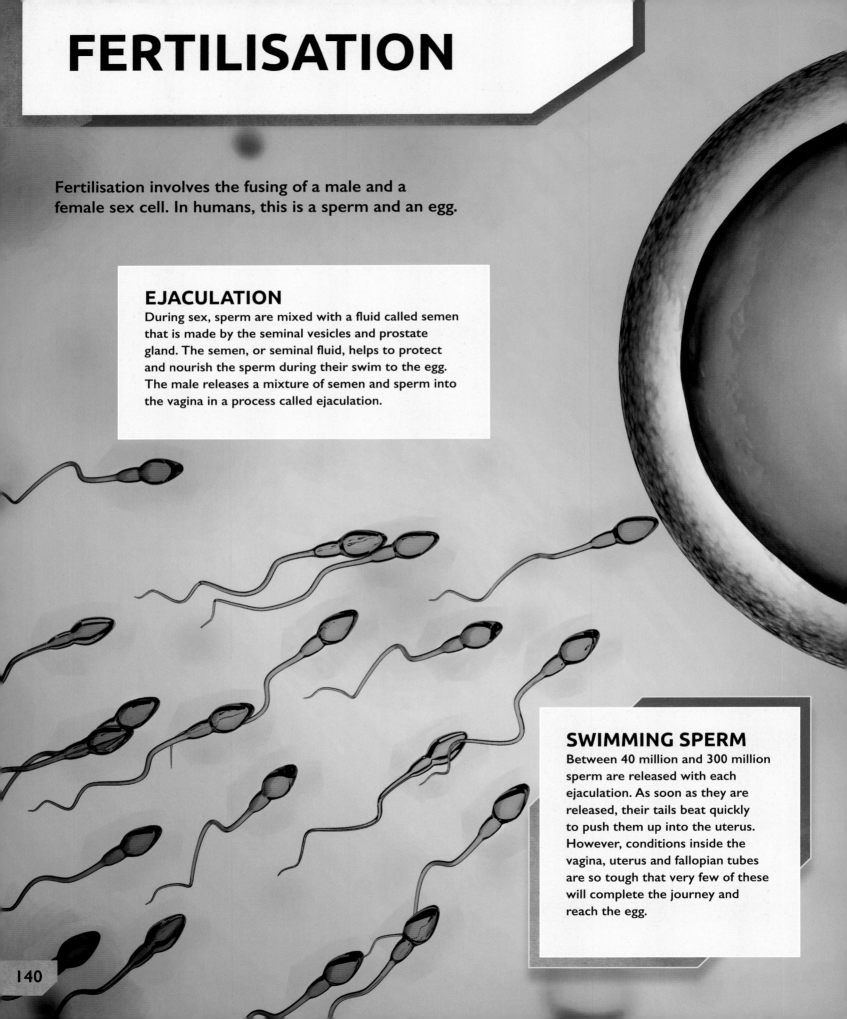

FERTILISATION

Fertilisation involves the fusing of a male and a female sex cell. In humans, this is a sperm and an egg.

EJACULATION

During sex, sperm are mixed with a fluid called semen that is made by the seminal vesicles and prostate gland. The semen, or seminal fluid, helps to protect and nourish the sperm during their swim to the egg. The male releases a mixture of semen and sperm into the vagina in a process called ejaculation.

SWIMMING SPERM

Between 40 million and 300 million sperm are released with each ejaculation. As soon as they are released, their tails beat quickly to push them up into the uterus. However, conditions inside the vagina, uterus and fallopian tubes are so tough that very few of these will complete the journey and reach the egg.

FERTILISATION

Once the sperm have reached the egg, their troubles haven't finished, as the outside of the egg is surrounded by three layers of protection. They use chemicals on their tips, or acrosome, and their pointed heads to burrow through the layers, while pushing forwards with their tails. As soon as one sperm breaks through the protection and reaches the egg membrane, the egg creates a chemical barrier that repels the other sperm, making it impenetrable. The genetic material from the successful sperm then merges with that in the egg and fertilisation is complete. The fertilised egg is now called a zygote and it continues its journey to the uterus.

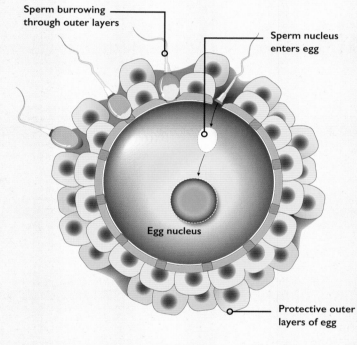

Sperm burrowing through outer layers

Sperm nucleus enters egg

Egg nucleus

Protective outer layers of egg

Before reaching an egg, these sperm will have swum up through the cervix, into the uterus and fallopian tubes.

TWINS

Identical twins are caused when the cells from one fertilised egg split and develop into two foetuses. Non-identical twins form when both ovaries release an egg at the same time and both are fertilised.

PREGNANCY AND BIRTH

During the nine months after fertilisation, the cell divides to form an embryo and then a foetus. The developing baby becomes bigger and stronger, nurtured by the mother until it is ready to be born.

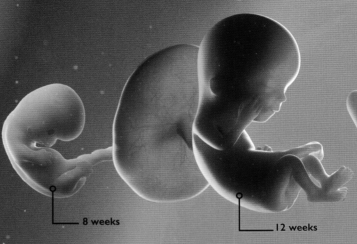

4 weeks

8 weeks

12 weeks

16 weeks

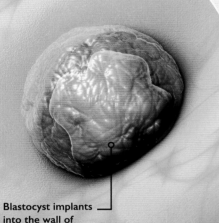

Blastocyst implants into the wall of the uterus.

4 WEEKS
The ball of cells is now called an embryo. Internal organs, including the lungs, stomach and liver start to develop along with the heart and blood vessels. External structures that will become the head, face and neck start to form.

8 WEEKS
The embryo is now about 1.5 cm (0.6 inches) long, eyelids and ears are forming. The arms and legs are well formed with the start of fingers and toes. At this stage it is referred to as a foetus.

12 WEEKS
Measuring about 5 cm (2 inches), the foetus starts to move.

16 WEEKS
The heart and blood vessels are fully formed and the foetus can blink its eyes and suck its thumb. It will be about 11.5 cm (4.5 inches) long.

14 DAYS
As it moves along the fallopian tube, the cells in the fertilized zygote divide over and over again, forming a hollow ball of cells called a blastocyst. When it reaches the uterus, the blastocyst implants itself into the thick lining of the uterus wall. Over the coming months, the cells develop to form recognisable features, including arms, legs and a head.

BELLY BUTTON
The remains of the umbilical cord drop off the newborn infant within the first two weeks. This leaves behind a small scar of skin which is your navel or belly button.

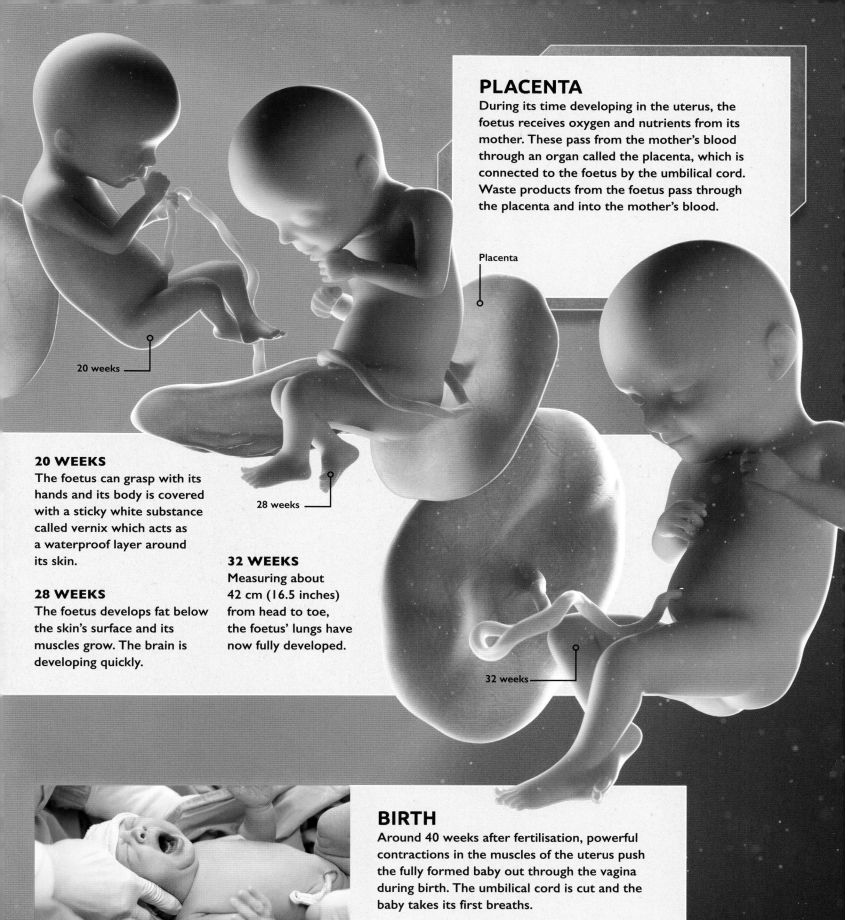

PLACENTA

During its time developing in the uterus, the foetus receives oxygen and nutrients from its mother. These pass from the mother's blood through an organ called the placenta, which is connected to the foetus by the umbilical cord. Waste products from the foetus pass through the placenta and into the mother's blood.

Placenta

20 weeks

28 weeks

32 weeks

20 WEEKS

The foetus can grasp with its hands and its body is covered with a sticky white substance called vernix which acts as a waterproof layer around its skin.

28 WEEKS

The foetus develops fat below the skin's surface and its muscles grow. The brain is developing quickly.

32 WEEKS

Measuring about 42 cm (16.5 inches) from head to toe, the foetus' lungs have now fully developed.

BIRTH

Around 40 weeks after fertilisation, powerful contractions in the muscles of the uterus push the fully formed baby out through the vagina during birth. The umbilical cord is cut and the baby takes its first breaths.

CHILDHOOD AND PUBERTY

The first years of life see a huge amount of growth in a human as they develop from a newborn infant, through childhood and into adolescence. During these years the child will develop the skills they need to see them into adult life.

INFANCY

A new baby is completely dependent on its parents. During the first few years, however, the baby's body will develop and grow rapidly and they start to develop and master skills such as talking and walking.

MOTHER'S MILK

Like all mammals, humans are able to feed their newborn children with milk produced by the mother's mammary glands, which are found in the breasts. The mammary glands develop during puberty, but they do not start to function until pregnancy. Just before a woman gives birth, hormones released by the pituitary gland start the production of milk from the mammary glands.

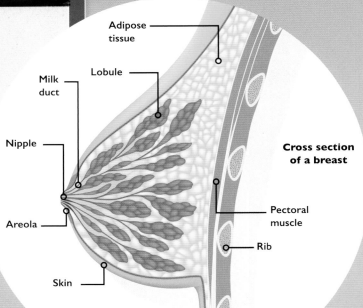

Adipose tissue

Lobule

Milk duct

Nipple

Cross section of a breast

Areola

Pectoral muscle

Rib

Skin

CHILDHOOD

During childhood, the body and brain continue to grow. The growing child develops more physical skills, including running, throwing and catching, and riding a bike, as well as mental abilities such as reading and writing.

PUBERTY

At the beginning of the teenage years, a child enters puberty. Sex hormones are produced in increasing levels, and these make the sex organs mature. There is also a rapid growth spurt, and hair grows in the armpits and around the genitals. Boys also start to grow hair on their faces and the pitch of their voice drops as their voices 'break'.

GROWING UP AND AGEING

Growing old is part of life. Once a person has reached their adult years, their body's abilities start to weaken and decline.

ADULTHOOD
Around the ages of 18–20, you stop growing as you reach adulthood. Around this time your body will reach its peak in terms of fitness and fertility. This lasts until the person reaches their mid-30s, when some of the body's activities start to slow and decline as the person heads towards old age.

Eating well and staying active and healthy can help to slow the effects of ageing.

THE EFFECTS OF AGEING

As you grow older, the body takes longer to replace and repair damaged parts and it starts to show the signs of old age. These include:

SKIN
Your skin becomes less elastic and starts to wrinkle.

HAIR
Your hair will start to thin and go grey.

TEETH
Your gums may pull back from your teeth and they can become more vulnerable to decay and infection.

EYES AND EARS
You may have trouble focussing on close objects and your hearing ability may decrease.

CIRCULATORY SYSTEM
Your blood vessels will lose elasticity, increasing the risk of high blood pressure.

BLADDER AND URINARY TRACT
Your bladder may become less elastic, resulting in the need to go to the toilet more often.

BONES, JOINTS AND MUSCLES
Your bones may shrink slightly and become less dense, making them more likely to fracture. Your muscles will start to lose strength, endurance and flexibility.

MEMORY AND THINKING
These may be affected by old age. For example, older adults may have trouble remembering someone's name or something that has just happened to them.

FIGHTING THE EFFECTS OF AGEING

While you can't stop the ageing process completely, there are things you can do to lessen its effects. Taking regular exercise will help to keep muscles strong and bones dense and your circulatory system healthy. It can also help you to stay mentally healthy. A good diet should include plenty of fresh fruit and vegetables, as well as fibre to keep your gut healthy, and minerals, such as calcium to keep bones dense. You should also keep mentally active by reading, playing intellectual games or taking up a hobby and keeping sociable, as interacting with other people helps to combat stress and depression, which can affect memory loss.

THE GENETIC CODE

The biological code that makes you a human (and what makes you you) is stored in a special molecule that's found inside the nucleus of every cell in your body (except for red blood cells). This molecule is called deoxyribonucleic acid, or DNA.

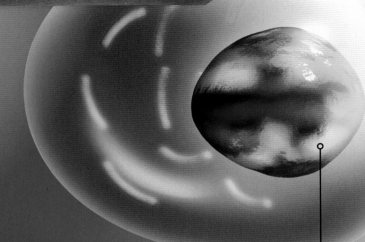

Cell nucleus

Chromosome

CELL CHROMOSOMES

Each cell nucleus contains two sets of 23 chromosomes – one set will have been inherited from the father and one set from the mother at fertilisation (see pages 140–141). These chromosomes contain the thousands of genes that give you your physical appearance and certain aspects of your character.

GENETIC SIMILARITY

You are about 99.9 per cent genetically similar to every other person on this planet. Over the billions of years of evolution, genetic information has changed greatly, but you still share the same genetic information with every other living thing on the planet.

The genetic similarity between a human and a chimpanzee is 96 per cent.

The genetic similarity between a human and a cat is 90 per cent.

The genetic similarity between a human and a banana is 60 per cent.

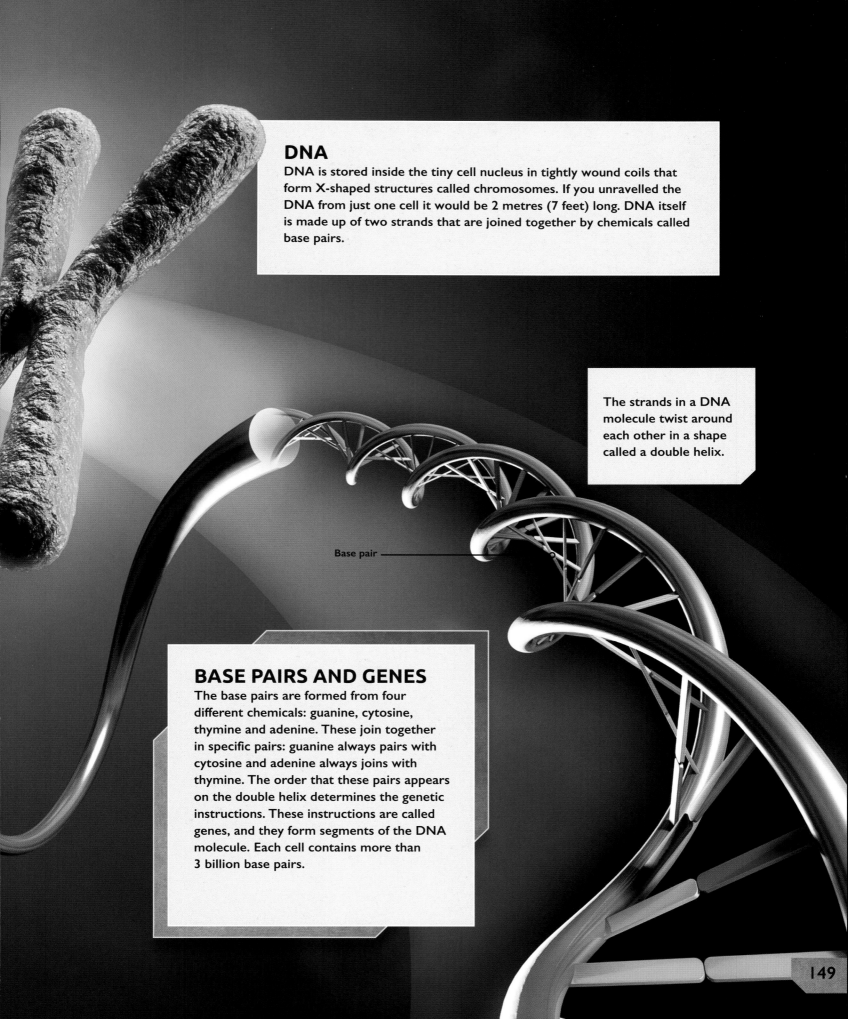

DNA

DNA is stored inside the tiny cell nucleus in tightly wound coils that form X-shaped structures called chromosomes. If you unravelled the DNA from just one cell it would be 2 metres (7 feet) long. DNA itself is made up of two strands that are joined together by chemicals called base pairs.

The strands in a DNA molecule twist around each other in a shape called a double helix.

Base pair

BASE PAIRS AND GENES

The base pairs are formed from four different chemicals: guanine, cytosine, thymine and adenine. These join together in specific pairs: guanine always pairs with cytosine and adenine always joins with thymine. The order that these pairs appears on the double helix determines the genetic instructions. These instructions are called genes, and they form segments of the DNA molecule. Each cell contains more than 3 billion base pairs.

INHERITANCE

Because you receive a set of genetic instructions from both your father and your mother, you also inherit some of their characteristics, including physical features and some aspects of how you behave.

SEX CELLS

The sex cells of the male and female each contain 23 chromosomes. At fertilisation, this genetic material merges to create the 46 chromosomes (23 pairs) found in each of your cells. Each set of chromosomes contains genes (one from each parent) for each characteristic that you inherit.

DOMINANT OR RECESSIVE?

Even though you inherit genes for each characteristic from both parents, one of these genes will be more influential than the other one. This is called the dominant gene, while the other, less-influential one is called the 'allele' gene. You will show the characteristics dictated by the dominant gene.

If one parent has recessive genes for blue eyes, and the other has dominant genes for brown eyes, then you will have brown eyes.

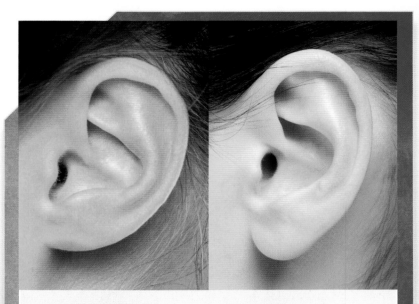

The earlobes on some people are attached to the sides of their heads (left), while others have unattached earlobes (right). This feature is inherited.

INHERITED FEATURES

Many of the features you inherit from your parents are quite obvious and they include eye colour, hair texture and colour, skin tone, blood group and freckles. However, there are a few that are less obvious. Whether your earlobes are attached to the side of your head or are unattached is inherited, as is sneezing in the presence of bright lights, whether or not you have sweaty palms, and even whether or not you suffer from insomnia and find sleeping difficult. Other inherited traits can include susceptibility to particular diseases, such as haemophilia, and other medical conditions.

Children inherit physical and behavioural features from their parents.

GLOSSARY

ALLERGIC REACTION: A sensitivity to a substance, called an allergen, which causes the body to trigger an overreaction by the body's immune system. For example, some people suffer from hay fever and are allergic to pollen. Contact with pollen can cause itchy eyes, runny nose and sneezing.

ALVEOLI: The air sacs that are found at the ends of the airways in the lungs. Oxygen passes through these and into the blood, while carbon dioxide travels in the other direction.

ANTAGONISTIC PAIRS: Refers to a pair of muscles that work in opposite directions to pull a body part back and forth.

ANTIBODY: A substance found in the blood that can recognise and attach itself to a specific antigen. The immune system can then recognise this antigen and attack and destroy it.

ANTIGEN: A foreign substance that triggers an immune response in the body.

ARTERY: A type of blood vessel that carries blood away from the heart. Arteries have thick, muscly walls to transport blood under high pressure.

AUTONOMIC NERVOUS SYSTEM: The part of the nervous system that controls body functions that you are unaware of for most of the time, such as breathing and heart rate.

AXONS: The part of a nerve cell that carries signals away from the cell body and to other nerve cells.

BILE: A liquid that helps with digestion and is produced by the liver and stored in the gall bladder.

BLASTOCYST: The ball of cells formed about five to six days after fertilisation. The cells inside the ball will go on to form the embryo.

CAPILLARY: A thin blood vessel or lymphatic vessel with walls that are usually only one cell thick.

CARBOHYDRATES: A type of food that is made up of carbon, hydrogen and oxygen. Carbohydrates include sugars, starch and cellulose.

CARDIAC MUSCLE: A type of muscle tissue that is only found in the heart.

CARTILAGE: A type of flexible connective tissue that supports some structures, such as the trachea and the external ear, and covers the bone surfaces in some joints.

CELL: The smallest functional unit in an organism.

CEREBELLUM: The part of the brain that sits at the back of the skull and controls and coordinates muscle movements.

CEREBROSPINAL FLUID: The liquid that sits around the brain and the spinal cord, cushioning and protecting them.

CEREBRUM: The topmost part of the brain. It is divided into two halves, or hemispheres, and is the largest part of the human brain.

CHROMOSOME: A long threadlike structure made of long strands of a single molecule of DNA found in the nucleus of a cell that contains genetic information.

CHYME: The fluid made up of partially digested food, acids and other chemicals that leaves the stomach and enters the small intestine.

COMPACT BONE: Also known as cortical bone, this is the dense tissue that forms the outer layer in bones throughout the body.

CORTEX: The outer layer of an organ, such as the brain and the kidneys.

DERMIS: The skin layer that sits below the epidermis and contains the blood vessels, sweat glands, hair follicles and nerve endings.

DIALYSIS: Cleaning the blood by passing it through a dialysis machine which replaces the functions of the kidneys.

DIGESTION: The breakdown of food into smaller substances, which can then be absorbed by the body.

DNA: Short for deoxyribonucleic acid, this is the long, threadlike chemical that stores the genetic information for an organism.

EJACULATION: The release of semen from the penis.

ENDOCRINE SYSTEM: The body system made up of glands and organs that release hormones.

ENZYME: A chemical that speeds up the rate of a chemical reaction, such as the digestion of food.

EPIDERMIS: The outer layer of the skin.

FAECES: Solid waste matter that is made up of unwanted food material and which leaves the body through the anus.

FATS: A type of foodstuff that is made up of glycerol and fatty acids. Fats include oils and butter.

FATTY ACIDS: A component of fats.

FERTILISATION: The fusing together of a male sex cell (sperm) and a female sex cell (egg).

FOLLICLE: A small sac or gland from which something grows, such as a hair follicle, or is released, such as an ovarian follicle.

FONTANELLE: A space between the skull bones of a newborn baby. These close up as the baby gets older.

FRACTURE: A partial or complete break in a bone.

GENE: A part of a DNA molecule which contains the genetic information for a particular characteristic.

GLAND: Part of the body which secretes a chemical substance. For example, sweat glands in the skin produce sweat to help cool the body.

GLYCEROL: A component of fats.

HORMONES: Special chemicals which, when released into the body, control the actions of certain body parts.

IMMUNISATION: Making someone immune to infection usually by giving them a vaccine.

INFECTION: The invasion and multiplication of germs such as bacteria or viruses within the body. Infections can cause ill effects and, in extreme cases, even death.

INTEGUMENTARY SYSTEM: The system that makes the outermost layer of the body, including the skin, hair and nails.

JOINTS: The points where two or more bones meet.

KERATIN: A tough protein that is found in hairs, nails and the outermost skin cells.

GLOSSARY

MARROW: The soft tissue that is found in the centre of many bones. Red bone marrow contains developing blood cells, while yellow bone marrow is mostly made up of fat.

MELANIN: A dark brown to black pigment that is found in the hair and skin and which gives these body parts their colouring. Melanin is released into the skin by exposure to sunlight, producing a sun tan.

MENSTRUATION: The release of blood and parts of the uterus lining by a woman that occurs usually once a month as part of the menstrual cycle.

MINERALS: Special substances that play a key role in keeping the body healthy and should form part of a balanced diet. For example, calcium is important in maintaining a strong skeleton.

MOTOR NERVE: A type of nerve that carries a signal from the brain or spinal cord to a body part.

MYELIN SHEATH: An insulating layer that wraps around many nerve cells, allowing them to send signals quickly and efficiently.

NEURON: Another name for a nerve cell.

NUTRIENTS: Substances found in food that play important roles in keeping the body fit and healthy. They could supply energy or other substances that the body can use to grow and repair itself.

ORGAN: A collection of different tissues to form an individual body part that carries out a specific function. Body organs include the brain, stomach and skin.

OSSICLES: The tiny bones that are found inside the ears and which transfer and amplify sound waves from the middle ear to the inner ear.

OVULATION: A stage in the menstrual cycle when an egg is released from an ovary.

PATHOGEN: Something that causes a disease, such as a bacterium or a virus.

PERISTALSIS: The wave of muscle contraction and relaxation that pushes food through the intestines.

PHAGOCYTOSIS: The process when a white blood cell envelops and destroys a pathogen.

PLASMA: The straw-coloured liquid that forms part of blood.

PLATELET: A small cell fragment that is found in blood and plays a key role in blood clotting.

PROPRIOCEPTION: The awareness of the body's position and movement.

PROSTHESIS: An artificial body part, such as an artificial leg or heart.

PROTEINS: A type of substance that is made up of amino acids and which forms an important part of a healthy diet. The body uses proteins for many of its most important processes, including building more cells and repairing damaged ones.

PUBERTY: The period triggered by the release of the sex hormones and when humans reach their sexual maturity.

REFLEX ACTIONS: The body's response to a stimulus, which is made automatically and without a conscious decision.

REM: Short for Rapid Eye Movement, this is a stage of sleep, when the eyes move about quickly and when most dreams occur.

RESPIRATION: The process in all living things, which releases energy, usually by combining oxygen and glucose to produce carbon dioxide, water and energy.

SEBACEOUS GLANDS: Small glands found in the skin that produce sebum, an oily substance that helps to keep skin and hair supple.

SENSORY NERVE: A type of nerve that carries signals from a sensor towards the spinal cord and brain.

SKELETAL MUSCLE: A type of muscle tissue that is connected to the bones and which helps to move the body around.

SMOOTH MUSCLE: A type of muscle tissue that is found in many internal organs, such as the intestines, and which is usually not under voluntary control.

SPHINCTER: A ring of muscle tissue that closes an opening or tube, such as the anus and the entry and exit to the stomach.

SPONGY BONE: A type of bone tissue that is porous and filled with red bone marrow. Spongy bone tissue helps to keep bones light but strong.

SYNAPSE: The space between two nerve cells.

SYNOVIAL JOINT: A type of joint, such as the hip or elbow, where the ends of the bones are surrounded by a capsule that contains synovial fluid to help the bones move smoothly.

SYSTEM: In the body, this is a collection of bones and tissues that work together to perform specific functions. Body systems include the skeletal, nervous and endocrine systems.

TISSUE: A collection of the same type of cell that work together as a unit.

TRANSFUSION: The transfer of blood from one person to another.

VACCINE: A substance that stimulates the production of antibodies and gives immunity from a disease.

VASOCONSTRICTION: The shrinking of blood vessels to divert blood away from part of the body.

VASODILATION: The enlarging of blood vessels to allow more blood to flow to a body part.

VEIN: A type of blood vessel that carries blood back to the heart. Veins have valves inside them to stop the low-pressure blood from flowing the wrong way.

VILLI: Tiny, fingerlike structures that increase the surface area of body parts, such as the intestines.

VIRUS: An infectious object that needs the cells of a living organism to replicate itself.

VITAMINS: A substance that is important for certain body functions. For example, vitamin D helps the body absorb calcium to produce strong bones.

X-RAYS: A high-energy form of energy that can pass through soft body parts, but is blocked by hard body parts such as bones. X-rays can be used to produce images of internal body parts.

INDEX

ACKNOWLEDGEMENTS

The publishers would like to thank the following sources for their kind permission to reproduce the pictures and footage in this book. The numbers listed below give the page on which they appear in the book.
(T=top, B=bottom, L=left, R=right, C=centre)

Alamy:
129tc IanDagnall Computing / Alamy Stock Photo

Shutterstock.com:
3 SciePro, 4-5 SciePro, 6t vipman, 6cl, b MattLphotography, 6c Designua, 7c metamorworks, 7t SciePro, 7tr, c sciencepics, 8–9 Alex Kravtsov, 10–11 Motionblur Studios, 10bl Rido, 11ct Creative Cat Studio, 11cb Tyler Olson, 11bl, br Sakurra, 12–13 Kateryna Kon, 12l Albert Kho, 13tr lonesomebunny, 13bl GraphicsRF.com, 14–15 Kjpargeter, 14cl Magic mine, 15cr , 15br Tatjana Baibakova, 16, 17cl, 17br SciePro, 17tc, 17bl sciencepics 17tr Veronika Surovtseva, 18cl Choksawatdikorn, 18bc Bborriss.67, 19t sciencepics, 19br vetpathologist, 20–21 Kateryna Kon, 20b studiovin, 21 beranicle, 22cl Vladimir Gjorgiev, 22r SciePro, 23t VectorMine, 23b Liliya Butenko, 24 SciePro, 24b Alexander_P, 25t nat20, 25br solomonphotos, 26cl SciePro, 26bl ilusmedical, 26–27 Lionel Alvergnas, 27tr MattLphotography, 27cr New Africa, 28l Blamb, 28–29 all VectorMine, 30–31t sciencepics, 30–31b BlueRingMedia, 31br Aldona Griskeviciene, 32–33 TreesTons, 32cl Pixel-Shot, 33tr 2shrimpS, 33br LightField Studios, 34t Designua, 34b udaix, 35all stihii, 36–37 Derya Cakirsoy, 36bl Tom Wang, 37tr Akarat Phasura, 37cr ILYA AKINSHIN, 37br Sahara Prince, 38-39 Hans Christiansson, 38bl ChooChin, 39cr BioMedical, 39bc SciePro, 40–41 YanLev, 42–43 beats1, 43tr Aliona Manakova, 44cr gritsalak karalak, 45 Liya Graphics, 46 Teguh Mujiono, 47t Elen Bushe, 47bl Siberian Art, 45cr kurhan, 48–49 SciePro, 48 cl and bl Alila Medical Media, 49cr sciencepics, 50–51 Rost9, 50 Liya Graphics, 51cr Andrea Danti, 52bl eranicle, 52–53 Tefi, 53t Nathan Devery, 54–55 Kateryna Kon, 54c Maxx-Studio, 55bl New Africa, 56cl Schira, 56–57 metamorworks, 57 VectorMine, 58–59 vipman, 60–61 t and c, 60b sciencepics, 62-63 goa novi, 62bl sciencepics, 63t Macrovector, 63cl JY FotoStock, 63br studiovin, 64, 65t, 65c sciencepics, 65b Khajornkiat Limsagul, 66–67, 66–67t SciePro, 66bl Alila Medical Media, 67cl first vector trend, 67br piccreative, 68–69b Alila Medical Media, 69tl Monkey Business Images, 69tr both Digitalpainto, 70–71 UfaBizPhoto, 70cl firatturgut, 70c Orange Deer studio, 70cr DKN0049 and Peter Hermes Furian, 70b Cast Of Thousands, 72–73 MattLphotography,

74r SciePro, 74bl picmedical, 75tl Systemoff, 75br Jacob Lund, 76–77 MattLphotography, 76br Tefi, 77br KateStudio, 78–79, 79tr SciePro, 78bl sciencepics, 79br grayjay, 80 SciePro, 81t Alex Mit, 81b Diana Creativa, 82 ducu59us, 83tl Polina MB, 83tr AnnaVel, 83c Krystyna Taran, 83bl fizkes, 83br DariaPotapova, 84 Magic3D, 85tc Daria Lixovetckay. 85tr Boyloso, 85cl Rawpixel.com, 85b Nolte Lourens, 86–87 fizkes, 87br SFIO CRACHO, 88–89 Jacob Lund, 88bl SciePro, 89tr KateStudio, 89b Ground Picture, 90cl Yaraslau Mikheyeu, 90tr Rose Carson, 90c Botond Horvath, 90bl Dragon Images, 90br Gorodenkoff, 91 PhawKStudio, 92–93 Alex Mit, 93t VectorMine, 93b BearFotos, 94cr Alhovik, 94cl pio3, 94–95b Ha-Yes Design, 95t LuckyBall, 95cr Perepadia Y, 96–97 Nemes Laszlo, 96 sciencepics, 97t trgrowth, 97c Kateryna Kon, 97br Howard Pimborough, 98–99 Nemes Laszlo, 98bl Designua, 98br Andrea Danti, 99tl Dionisvera. 99tcl Roman Samokhin, 99tc nortongo, 99tcr Photoongraphy, 99tr Tanya Sid, 99br Rigelp, 100–101 Axel_ Kock, 101br Eric Isselee, 102 Macrovector, 103tr Aigars Reinholds, 103cl Andrii Spy_k, 103b medicalstocks, 104–105 RFarrarons, 104c maxcreatnz, 105t Igor Samoiliuk, 105cr DarioZg, 106 Nerthuz, 107 Alila Medical Media, 108–109 Kateryna Kon, 109tc sciencepics, 109tr Liya Graphics, 109cl TreesTons, 109c JY FotoStock, 109cr Alila Medical Media, 109bl Alex Mit, 109bc Creative Cat Studio, 109br Tefi, 110–111 MattLphotography, 110c Sakurra, 110b Andrea Danti, 111br Andrey_Popov, 112 SciePro, 113t swissmacky, 114–115 Corona Borealis Studio, 116–117 Gustavo Tabosa, 116bl Juan Gaertner, 117cr Sorapop Udomsri, 117bl Marcos Mesa Sam Wordley, 118–119 somersault1824, 119tr Alexander Sobol, 120r Hank Grebe, 120bl Aldona Griskeviciene, 121tl Lightspring, 121tr Inna Kharlamova, 121c Designua, 122c all Puwadol Jaturawutthichai, 122–123 Luca9257, 124-125 Corona Borealis Studio, 124br Kateryna Kon, 126-127 sruilk, 126br Kateryna Kon, 127tr ajlatan, 127c BigTunaOnline, 127bl Pixel-Shot, 127br Rob Byron, 128bl Zwiebackesser, 128br J J Osuna Caballero, 129tr nobeastsofierce, 129bl Everett Collection, 129br Jezper, 130–131 Prostock-studio, 130bl Everett Collection, 132–133 sportpoint, 132cl Max4e Photo, 133cr ChaNaWiT, 134-135 SciePro, 136c, 137c Macrovector, 136b Cinemanikor, 137b SciePro, 138–139 KateStudio, 138bl pr_camera, 139br Alina Kruk, 140–141 koya979, 141cr Designua, 141b Shen max, 142cl Christoph Burgstedt, 142–143 all SciePro, 143b Mongaman, 144cr sirtravelalot, 144cl Kingspirit Image Room, 144br Tsuyna, 145l KK Tan, 145r Dean Drobot, 146–147 LightField Studios, 148–149 Andrea Danti, 148cl Dr. Norbert Lange, 148bl Pixfiction, 148bcl Happy Author, 148bcr Eric Isselee, 148br Djomas, 150–151 Rido, 150br Serg Zastavkin, 151tc BLACKDAY, 151tr Tatjana Romanova